BOB'S
RULES OF ORDER

---

for Colorado Local Governments

BOB'S
RULES OF ORDER

for Colorado Local Governments

SIMPLIFIED PARLIAMENTARY RULES
FOR PUBLIC MEETINGS

PEAK NINE
PRESS

ROBERT C. WIDNER

Publisher: Peak Nine Press LLC. connect@peakninepress.com

Special Thanks to:

Widner Juran LLP for assistance with experience, ideas, research, editing, and review. Widner Juran LLP 13133 East Arapahoe Road, Suite 100, Centennial, Colorado 80112

The Colorado Municipal League (CML) for support in the preparation, printing, and distribution of *Bob's Rules*. CML 1144 Sherman Street, Denver, Colorado 80203. cml.org

Printed and bound in the United States of America. Denver, Colorado.

ISBN: 979-8-9878358-6-9   (Print)
         979-8-9878358-0-7   (eBook)

Bob's Rules of Order does not provide legal advice. This publication is a source of information for the reader and is not meant as a substitute for legal counsel. Please contact your attorney for assistance.

An Open Invitation

Bob's Rules of Order will be periodically updated through new editions as efficient meeting practices become known and to correct or supplement the *Rules*. The author invites anyone using *Bob's Rules* to pose questions, offer ideas, and make suggestions to improve the *Rules* to serve our shared goal of serving the public through our local governments.

TABLE OF CONTENTS

Chapter 4

POINTS AND MOTIONS GENERALLY

Chapter 5

THE POINTS

Chapter 6

THE MOTIONS

Chapter 7

EXECUTIVE SESSIONS

Chapter 8

APPOINTMENT AND ELECTION PROCESSES

Additional Information

Appendices

PREFACE

Sitting in countless public meetings for a variety of local governments over more than 30 years, I noted that many governments formally adopted *Robert's Rules of Order* to govern their meetings. Other governments never formally adopted rules of order but nevertheless referred to *Robert's Rules* as their guiding rules of order.

However, none of the local governments followed all the requirements of *Robert's Rules*. Instead, they followed practices based on what they believed *Robert's Rules* required. The governments proposed and seconded motions, engaged in discussion and debate, and voted on motions. They followed only a small part of *Robert's Rules*. In doing so, they unknowingly ignored many of the rules' specific requirements or they incorporated practices and procedures into their meetings that directly conflicted with the requirements of *Robert's Rules*. Admittedly, these practices and procedures worked because the governments accomplished their business. It was the successful meeting practices based on a belief of what *Robert's Rules* required, and the deviations from *Robert's Rules*, that served as the genesis of *Bob's Rules of Order*.

Bob's Rules of Order is based on some of the commonly accepted ideas, methods, and procedures first offered by *Robert's Rules* in 1876. In this regard, *Bob's Rules* may not be entirely original or innovative. I trust, however, that local governments will view *Bob's Rules* as original and innovative due to its tailoring of rules and procedures to the specific needs of Colorado local governments. I know of no uniform or standardized set of meeting rules tailored to the common practices and special needs of Colorado local government. It is this void that *Bob's Rules of Order* hopes to fill.

Lastly, *Bob's Rules* is my attempt to support what I believe to be the most efficient and responsible form of government. I am continually impressed by the unwavering dedication of local governments in serving the needs of citizens. No other form of government does more with the taxpayers' dollars, and no other government, in my view, cares as directly and personally about the welfare of its citizens. It is my hope that *Bob's Rules of Order* can aid in the continuing success of our local governments well into the future.

Bob Widner

INTRODUCTION

Public meetings are critically important to local government. Often, a public meeting is a citizen's only opportunity to directly observe the workings of their government.

An efficient meeting allows all scheduled business to be accomplished, voices to be fairly and equitably heard, and differences of opinion to be aired amicably. Whether the issues at hand are challenging and evoke intense emotion or they are simply administrative and non-confrontational, a well-run meeting leaves all participants feeling that the decisions made during the meeting were the products of organization, fairness, equity, and respect. An efficient and well-run public meeting can aid in building the public's confidence and trust in local government.

A poorly run meeting displays a degree of dysfunction that causes citizens to believe that all aspects of the government are equally dysfunctional. Such a meeting can also lead to inequity among participants when engaged in discussion and debate, create conflict and argument between the participants, and inject confusion into the decision-making process. In short, a poorly run meeting may result in decisions that appear to lack a thorough evaluation of the issues while also undermining the public's confidence and trust in local government.

Rules of order[1] are vital to an efficient public meeting. They provide processes and procedures that are pre-designed to create organization, to promote fairness among participants, and to lead to a more thorough evaluation of the issues raised at the meeting. In doing so, they lead to more justifiable and supportable decisions.

Local government rules of order must be carefully prepared. The rules must demonstrate an understanding of the local government's specialized purpose and recognize the specialized laws that limit and guide the exercise of the government's authority.

Rules of order that are overly complex will not be consistently followed and can prove to be ineffective in the conduct of a meeting. Rules of order that are easily understandable with a scope appropriate for the actions customarily undertaken by the decision-making body will more than likely be routinely followed by meeting participants. When routinely followed over longer periods of time, the rules become an accepted part of the fabric of the decision-making process and will readily survive future changes in the membership of the decision-making body.

Robert's Rules Of Order

When considering the possible adoption of a set of meeting rules, *Robert's Rules of Order* is often a suggested starting point. *Robert's Rules* is the most widely known set of general parliamentary[2] rules.

Robert's Rules of Order is a remarkable work. Beginning with the pocket handbook first published in 1876, and with significant rewriting and amendment since that time, *Robert's Rules of Order*[3] evolved into a complex tool for meeting management.[4] The 12th edition of *Robert's Rules* totals 803 pages[5] and offers 98 motions[6] and dozens of procedural rules, many of which are subject to exceptions. At least two dozen publications are available to help meeting participants better understand, interpret, clarify, and decipher *Robert's Rules*, including a *Robert's Rules for Dummies*[7] and a *Complete Idiot's Guide to Robert's Rules*.[8] Several websites are also available, offering various and sometimes conflicting opinions on the proper application of *Robert's Rules*.

Although *Robert's Rules* are available for use in meetings of all types, the typical local government meeting does not benefit from complex rules. The business of local government is to get business done. The business of local government is not to engage in debate about the appropriate application of 98 motions and 803 pages of rules.

Most importantly, *Robert's Rules* does not incorporate the specialized meeting mandates and requirements imposed upon local government by the state's legislature, local charters, and local laws. *Robert's Rules* provides no aid to local governments in meeting the obligations of the Colorado Open Meetings Law. And the largest shortcoming of *Robert's Rules* is its lack of recognition of the specialized nature and needs of the quasi-judicial process that many local government bodies must follow. *Robert's Rules* mentions the term "quasi-judicial" when identifying that certain boards have different duties, but it offers no processes or procedures designed to manage a quasi-judicial hearing.

Robert's Rules of Order is not a suitable resource to manage the common local government meeting, with an exception for the most sophisticated and largest of governmental bodies exclusively engaged in legislative decision making. *Robert's Rules* is most suitable for an exceptionally large deliberative or legislative body where a knowledgeable, experienced, or certified[9] meeting parliamentarian can direct the meeting in compliance with the rules. Again, *Robert's Rules* is a remarkable work for such a purpose.

Notwithstanding the shortcomings of *Robert's Rules of Order*, many local governments have formally adopted *Robert's Rules* for their local parliamentary procedure. The decision to adopt *Robert's Rules* is rarely the result of a comprehensive understanding of its requirements and a deliberate determination that the rules will mesh with local needs. Instead, the decision to adopt *Robert's Rules* often assumes that the rules will best guide meeting procedure because the rules are a widely known set of parliamentary rules. And, unfortunately, there are no other parliamentary rules specifically designed for local government meetings.[10]

For those local governments that have adopted *Robert's Rules of Order*, it is troubling that few of the local government officials or administrative staff have read *Robert's Rules*. Even fewer know that *Robert's Rules* contains processes and procedures that the local government might find unacceptable,[11] that may be deemed overly complex and inconsistent with commonly accepted local meeting practices,[12] or that conflict with the laws applicable to local government meetings.[13] Equally troubling is that the local officials are rarely provided a copy of *Robert's Rules*, that *Robert's Rules* is rarely available for reference during a meeting, and that *Robert's Rules* is rarely cited during a meeting. Colorado local governmental bodies purporting to use *Robert's Rules* follow a process that they believe to be consistent with *Robert's Rules* but which, in practice, is not.

Other Meeting Rules of Order

Along with *Robert's Rules of Order*, there exist another dozen or more published handbooks and manuals available to guide meetings.[14] The vast majority of these publications recite the provisions of *Robert's Rules* and attempt to simplify *Robert's Rules*. The stated goal for many of these publications is to deliver a universally applicable set of rules available for use for all types of meetings, large and small. Nevertheless, these publications often caution that the rules must be modified—or even ignored—to address meetings of specialized bodies or to address special provisions of law. This caution is warranted for local governments because these various sets of purportedly uniformly applicable rules, as with *Robert's Rules*, do not demonstrate an understanding of the challenges and the legal requirements of the local government public meeting.

CHAPTER 1

BOB'S RULES OF ORDER

The Purpose of *Bob's Rules of Order*

Bob's Rules of Order for Colorado Local Governments implements the recognized authority of local governments to enact their own rules to manage the conduct of meetings.[15] Additionally, *Bob's Rules* is intended to serve as a tailored and, when compared to *Robert's Rules of Order*, a more simplified set of parliamentary rules designed specifically to meet the needs of Colorado local government. The *Rules* reflect the basic ideas and methods historically ingrained within meeting practices by the original 1876 version of *Robert's Rules*. Most importantly, *Bob's Rules* limits the available motions to those essential to advance the goal of running a more organized and efficient local government meeting.

Bob's Rules is prepared for use by the governing bodies of the various forms of local government—the city council or the board of trustees for home rule and statutory municipalities and the board of county commissioners for counties. *Bob's Rules* may also directly aid the various supporting and advisory boards, commissions, and committees of local government that engage in formal decision making, such as the planning and zoning commission, board of adjustment, board of review, and the various types of local licensing authorities. Special districts, governmental authorities, and quasi-governments may also find the use of *Bob's Rules* beneficial subject to changes to address any special needs of those organizations.

Applicability to Video Conferencing or "Remote Meetings"

Beginning with the COVID pandemic in 2020, various online video conferencing platforms, such as Zoom, Microsoft Teams, Adobe Connect, GoToMeeting, and Facebook Messenger, gained significant popularity and achieved widespread use in conducting local government meetings. Due to this popularity, as well as the ease of use and convenience to citizens, it is not anticipated that the use of online video conferencing platforms will diminish. Many local governments have included video conferencing (also called remote or virtual meetings) in the available options for holding public meetings.

The use of *Bob's Rules of Order* is compatible with a video conference meeting format.[16] These meetings provide an online meeting room in which people from remote locations can assemble and engage in two-way communication. The format of a video conference meeting is not significantly different than the in-person meeting historically used by local government.

Admittedly, a video conference meeting presents challenges for the Presiding Officer when managing fair access to the meeting's microphone by multiple parties, and the meeting is highly dependent on the successful operation of the software application and audio-visual equipment supporting the meeting. Video conference meetings can be less formal when compared to an in-person meeting due to the ability to easily leave the virtual meeting room or hide from view and to engage in multitasking. Notwithstanding these challenges, the rules and practices offered by *Bob's Rules of Order* will enable the Body in a video conference meeting to efficiently accomplish public business. One might argue that, because the interactions among participants in a video conference meeting can be more difficult for the Presiding Officer to manage, the use of rules of order that will guide the

Members' conduct is even more necessary for a video conference than an in-person meeting.

The Benefit of Rules of Order

Rules of order assist in enhancing fairness among meeting participants, providing necessary support when defending the decision-making process, and promoting meeting efficiency.

Fairness and Transparency

It is an unquestionable goal of local government to be fair in the administration of governmental powers, programs, and affairs. Fairness is an important element in the protection of the public's confidence in government. Moreover, providing fairness to meeting participants is a constitutional obligation imposed on government by procedural due process.[17] Fairness exists where similarly situated persons are treated in a similar fashion. Written rules of order, when consistently applied, will best advance the goal of fair treatment of all meeting participants.

The fairness provided by using pre-established rules of order adds transparency to the decision-making process. Considering agenda items in an improvised or ad hoc manner will appear to the public as arbitrarily applying different rules to different persons and to different issues. Decisions made informally can also appear to the public as the likely product of negotiation between the decision makers outside of the public meeting or hearing. In contrast, a decision reached through a somewhat formal, consistent, and uniform application of pre-established rules of order will often be viewed as extending fair and equal treatment to each of the matters presented to the Body.

Rules provide fairness to the Members of the decision-making Body. Some Colorado governments have not adopted formal rules to guide decision making. These governments render decisions through a largely informal process that, after some unstructured discussion, culminates in a motion placed before the Members for a vote. Perhaps not apparent to the meeting participants, the informal and "rule-less" process involves one or a few of the Members exercising greater control or power over the decision-making process. The more vocal, the more assertive, and the more experienced Members can often dominate the discussion and debate. The unstructured meeting can lead to confusion among the Members as to "what we should do next" and will oftentimes allow the Presiding Officer to exercise an inappropriate degree of control and influence over the meeting processes and the meeting outcome.

The absence of procedural rules can effectively quiet Members' voices. The Presiding Officer maintains significant power to control the Members' access to the Floor. In the absence of rules that protect the Members' right to the Floor, the Presiding Officer can ignore a Member's request to address the Body. And, absent a rule recognizing a right of appeal of the Presiding Officer's decisions, there is no recourse for the Member who feels disenfranchised by a decision of the Presiding Officer. Written rules that confer upon the Members of the Body an equal opportunity to participate in a meeting can inject into the decision-making process a greater degree of fairness.

Defending the Decision-Making Process

Along with fairness, rules are necessary to ensure legally defensible decisions. Government must always act in accordance with the law, and the law is invariably written.[18] When government acts in accordance with the law, which includes the rules that govern the government's meeting processes, it is a straightforward exercise to determine whether the government complied with the law. Compliance with procedural rules will oftentimes lead to the finding of a valid and enforceable action or decision, and, conversely, where there exists no law that authorizes the government's procedure, the government's action will be subject to challenge.[19] Written rules that support each procedural action undertaken by government serve an important, if not legally necessary, purpose.

Efficiency

Meeting efficiency is an obvious result of the consistent application of written rules of order. By following written rules designed to move the Body from introduction of an issue to a final decision, the Body will more often "stay on track" during the meeting.

It is inefficient for Members to repeatedly ask about the proper process to follow in each situation, to question or debate the appropriateness or suitability of a proposed unwritten practice, or to delay or postpone a decision to determine whether a particular process has been followed in the past in a similar circumstance.

Written rules allow the Members of the Body to understand that there is a pre-determined and accepted process for the meeting. Members will each know "what's next" as the decision-making process unfolds. The consistent use of pre-approved rules enables the Members to focus not on the process but on the information, discussion, and debate that can lead to an acceptable decision. Written rules offer greater process certainty and, as a result, greater meeting efficiency.

The Need for Some Flexibility

Most local governments do not operate comfortably or effectively in the face of rigid and inflexible procedural requirements. A local government meeting will often involve a degree of unanticipated or unforeseen situations that require deviation from an accepted rule. In addition, rigid and inflexible adherence to rules can undermine the Body's camaraderie and collaboration and may allow the Body's more educated or experienced Members to use strict rule application to control or stifle the participation of other Members. A degree of flexibility in the rules can help aid meeting efficiency when the flexibility will not diminish the quality of the decision-making process.

Bob's Rules of Order provides some flexibility and seeks to enhance efficiency by the following processes or procedures:

✦ The Presiding Officer maintains the discretion to unilaterally forgo or modify a rule and to take actions to improve the efficiency of the meeting subject to a Point of Order or Point of Appeal. See Rule 3.4.

✦ A formally stated motion is not always necessary, and a Member may instead use the exclamation "so moved" as an abbreviated form of motion. See Rule 5.1.

✦ A "Friendly Amendment" of a debatable motion is authorized, which would allow the Presiding Officer to forgo a formal Motion to Amend in the absence of an objection by a Member. See Rule 6.1.

✦ A "Friendly Withdrawal" of a debatable motion is authorized to allow for the informal removal of the motion from the Floor in the absence of an objection by a Member. See Rule 6.2.

✦ Suspending the application of certain rules is authorized at the discretion of the Presiding Officer or upon approval of a motion by the Body for any given agenda item or for the entire meeting. See Rules 8.1 and 8.2.

✦ The Body's deviation from a rule is deemed authorized when the deviation is inadvertent and non-substantive and does not receive an objection from a Member. See Rule 8.3.

Integration with Bylaws

It is important to recognize both the difference and the interplay between rules of order and what may be commonly known as the Body's "bylaws" or the principal policies governing the Body.[20] Bylaws, which may be known by many different titles[21] and which may include requirements of state law and home rule charters, are the government's local written ordinances, resolutions, or policies prepared for the purpose of governing the Body's purpose, structure, leadership, and organization. Bylaws are tailored to the specific purposes and needs of the Body. The bylaws for most local government bodies will typically address many of the following topics:

+ The purpose of the Body.

+ The voting membership and any alternate membership of the Body.

+ Identification of the Body's officers and the officers' duties.

+ Identification of support staff (clerk, attorney) and associated roles.

+ Types of authorized meetings (regular, special, study session, etc.).

+ Form of meetings (in person, telephonic, remote, or hybrid[22]).

+ Agenda preparation.

+ Meeting and hearing procedures and processes.

+ Consent agenda availability and process for approval.

+ Adoption of rules of order for decision making.

+ The public's opportunity to speak to the Body.

+ Rules or guidelines to protect meeting decorum.

+ Specialized public notice requirements for meetings.

+ Quorum requirements.

✦ Voting methods (i.e., use of roll call or voting machines).

✦ Recording and taking of minutes.

✦ Member attendance requirements and excused absences.

✦ Conflicts of interest and appearances of impropriety.

✦ Removal of a Member from the Body.

✦ Creation of and requirements for committees and subcommittees.

✦ Other matters to guide the Body's effective operation.

Given the differences between governmental bodies, it may be a rare instance that two sets of bylaws will be identical. Bodies differ as to their purpose, authority, composition, and resources, thereby necessitating bylaws that are tailored to each Body. Bylaws are typically not interchangeable for use between different bodies.

In contrast to bylaws, rules of order are the specific procedures necessary to open, consider, debate, and decide a matter presented to a Body. Because rules of order focus on the basic or common process for decision making (motion, debate, voting), the same set of rules of order can be used by different decision-making bodies.

Rules of order may, however, implicate or relate to matters addressed in the bylaws. For example, both the bylaws and the rules of order may address various aspects of voting. Bylaws may address the circumstances that constitute a conflict of interest, while the rules of order may direct that a Member with a conflict of interest may not vote on a motion. Also, bylaws will set the Body's quorum requirement for each type of meeting, and the rules of order will define how the absence of a quorum will affect the ability to hold a meeting or to consider an agenda item.

One key difference between bylaws and rules of order is the ease by which these two documents may be changed or their requirements suspended. Bylaws cannot be easily suspended on a case-by-case basis because the bylaws set forth the principal policies and critical controls over the Body's exercise of its authority. In a sense, the bylaws "hardwire" the key requirements of the Body's organizational structure and its authority. As an example, the Body cannot decide on a case-by-case basis to summarily suspend the bylaw requirements concerning a conflict of interest or to adjust the quorum requirement for a particular agenda item. These matters are essential or basic requirements for the Body's exercise of its power and authority. Rules of order, on the other hand, may be changed or suspended more readily to accommodate a specialized question, situation, or issue presented to the Body during the consideration of a matter—that is, if the rules of order accommodate such change or suspension.

Although they serve different purposes, there is a direct interplay or connection between the bylaws and rules of order. The bylaws will adopt a recognized set of procedural rules of order for use by the Body in its decision-making process, such as *Bob's Rules of Order*. The adopted rules of order, in turn, may authorize the Body to use a Point of Order and, as to any Presiding Officer's decision, a Point of Appeal to ensure that the Body follows the applicable provisions of the bylaws. See Sections 11.0 and 13.0.

How *Bob's Rules* May Change Current Meeting Practices

Because *Bob's Rules of Order* incorporates many of the common meeting practices of many Colorado local governments, there may not be significant changes for most local government bodies in the local practices following the adoption of *Bob's Rules*. However, there are some rules or procedures offered by *Bob's Rules* that, for some local governments, may present a change.

Most notably among the potential changes in terminology, rules, or practices would be the following:

+ Principal Motion. Many local rules of order, as well as *Robert's Rules of Order*, employ the phrase "main motion" to identify the motion that offers to the Body a general proposition or question to be decided.[23] The phrase "main motion" is also used by *Robert's Rules* to classify other motions for purposes of priority.[24] This dual and inconsistent use of the phrase "main motion" can result in confusion.

  Bob's Rules seeks to avoid this confusion by limiting the use of the phrase "main motion" to the determination of a motion's classification and its priority. Then, *Bob's Rules* employs the phrase "Principal Motion" to refer to a general business motion. See Section 9.0, Class and Priority of Motions, and Section 15.0, Principal Motion.

+ So Moved Motion. Some local governments allow a Member to quickly propose a motion by the expression "so moved." This practice is available where all Members of the Body readily understand the purpose and scope of the motion based on the immediately preceding discussion. However, for most local governments, the So Moved Motion is entertained without any formal rule authorizing the practice. *Bob's Rules* formally authorizes this practice subject to limits to ensure efficiency. See Rule 5.1.

+ Friendly Amendment. *Bob's Rules* recognizes the informal practice used by some local governments of a "Friendly Amendment." A Friendly Amendment is a simplified means of amending a debatable motion. The Friendly Amendment is an alternative to the use of a formal Motion to Amend. See Rule 6.1 and Section 17.0.

✦ Friendly Withdrawal. *Bob's Rules* authorizes the Body to forgo the need for a formal motion to withdraw a debatable motion from the Floor and instead authorizes the use of a "Friendly Withdrawal." Consistent with its use by some local governmental bodies, the Friendly Withdrawal is available when it is evident to the entire Body that the pending debatable motion is no longer needed or useful in reaching a decision. See Rule 6.2.

✦ Discussion Allowed Without a Motion on the Floor. Some local governmental bodies follow the mandate of *Robert's Rules of Order* that no substantive discussion may proceed without a formal motion on the Floor. Because this mandate is inconsistent with the exceedingly common practice of most local governmental bodies and can be counterproductive, *Bob's Rules* authorizes, but does not require, discussion without a formal motion. See Rule 1.5.

✦ Presiding Officer Discretion and Unanimous Consent. *Bob's Rules* authorizes the Presiding Officer to exercise discretion in making decisions during the conduct of the meeting. Absent an objection from a Member (that is, where there is unanimous consent by the Body), the Presiding Officer's decision will be effective. As for all decisions by the Presiding Officer, a Point of Order or Point of Appeal can formally challenge the Presiding Officer's compliance with the *Rules*. In addition, a simple objection from one Member can deny the Presiding Officer the authority to approve the use of the So Moved Motion, a Friendly Amendment, or a Friendly Withdrawal. See Rules 5.1, 6.1, and 6.2.

Incorporating *Bob's Rules* into Meeting Practice

Starting Point – Legal and Other Advice

When deciding to adopt rules of order to guide meetings, local governments should first seek the advice of their local legal counsel.

The local legal counsel is best suited to understand how any proposed procedural rules will coordinate with the laws affecting the local government, the government's common or historic meeting practices, and the special needs of the Body. It is not a best practice to blindly adopt or apply *Bob's Rules* without consulting the government's legal counsel.

The advice and counsel of the experienced local government clerk, manager, or administrator is also important. Clerks, managers, and administrators can provide invaluable insight into the historical practices of the local government and can highlight potential practice issues and conflicts arising from the implementation of new procedural rules.

Adoption of *Bob's Rules*

Bob's Rules of Order is available for incorporation into the local government Body's meeting practice. Where the local government has yet to adopt bylaws or another policy governing meetings, *Bob's Rules* may be adopted by either a resolution or an ordinance, depending on the advice of the Body's legal counsel.[25]

Where the local government previously adopted bylaws or another policy document governing the Body's organization and operation, the bylaws or policy document can adopt *Bob's Rules* by simple reference in the bylaws or policy. The reference can also address potential conflicts between the bylaws and the adopted rules of order. This reference might be stated as:

> *Bob's Rules of Order for Colorado Local Governments* (2023) is adopted as the rules of order for meetings of the [insert name of the Body]. In cases where the adopted edition of *Bob's Rules of Order* is inconsistent with these bylaws

and local rules of procedure, the bylaws and local rules of procedure shall govern and control.

Although *Bob's Rules* can be adopted without change or modification, its rules are not intended to be adopted without the local government's careful review of the appropriateness of the *Rules* for local meeting practices.

As a recommended process for the consideration and possible adoption of *Bob's Rules of Order*, the Body may wish to follow the ensuing procedure:

✦ The Body or a subcommittee of the Body, together with key administrative staff (a "Rules Committee"), should meet to review the entirety of *Bob's Rules of Order*. The Rules Committee should start with the basic question of whether *Bob's Rules* is generally appropriate for the Body's use and will be an improvement over the current adopted meeting procedures.

✦ If there is initial interest in incorporating the use of *Bob's Rules* into the Body's meeting practice, the Rules Committee should consider whether the Body currently follows or uses a form of each rule, point, and motion and, if so, whether the Body's current procedure is consistent with or deviates from the rule, point, or motion. The Rules Committee should identify any modifications or deletions of any rule, point, or motion that would best serve the Body's meeting practices[26] should the *Rules* be adopted.

✦ Following a complete review of *Bob's Rules*, the Rules Committee should determine whether *Bob's Rules*, with any needed modifications or deletions, should be recommended to the Body for adoption. Additionally, a determination should be made whether any modifications or revisions to any previously adopted bylaws are necessary to ensure harmony between the bylaws and the adopted *Rules*.

✦ If adoption of *Bob's Rules* is recommended by the Rules Committee, the Body's legal counsel should be consulted to recommend a procedure or method for adoption. The adopting document should include any identified modifications or deletions to the rules, points, and motions necessary to meet the Body's needs.[27]

✦ The adopting document should be presented to the appropriate Body or official authorized to adopt rules of procedure for the Body.

Training and Education

Together with formal incorporation of *Bob's Rules of Order* into meeting practice, the Members of each Body and any administrative and legal staff who will assist the Body in the use of the rules must necessarily understand the operation of the *Rules*.

It is hoped that *Bob's Rules* is sufficiently simplified that, after one or two thorough readings, a Member will understand the basics and, with time and practice, will become fully versed in the proper application of the *Rules*. Admittedly, procedural rules of order are not scintillating reading material. As a result, some more active introduction and training may be necessary to assist Members in the effective use of *Bob's Rules*.

A recommended process for training Members of a Body and administrative staff may include the following steps:

✦ A personal copy of *Bob's Rules* should be provided to each Member of the Body and each supporting staff member who may assist in the meeting process.

+ Each Member of the Body and each staff member should thoroughly read the *Rules* once and, based on a self-assessment of comprehension and understanding, possibly read the *Rules* again.

+ The Presiding Officer (and the Body's designated parliamentarian if the role is assigned to another person) should study the *Rules* in depth and gain a comprehensive and working knowledge of all rules and processes.

+ Members should engage in discussion and roleplaying involving meeting scenarios facilitated by either the Presiding Officer or a staff member well acquainted with the *Rules of Order*. These roleplaying and "walk-through" exercises can allow the Body to gain experience and confidence in the application of the *Rules*.

+ Training should emphasize the discretion afforded the Presiding Officer and the use of the primary points (Order and Information), as well as the motions that will be most frequently used by the Body. These motions include the Principal Motion, the So Moved Motion, the Motion to Amend, the Motion to Continue or Postpone, the Friendly Amendment and Friendly Withdrawal, and the Motion for Executive Session.

+ Following formal adoption of the *Rules*, the Body should take opportunities to review sections of the *Rules* when time permits during meetings. In addition, it may prove helpful for the Body's legal counsel or other senior staff member to debrief the Body regarding the successes and deficiencies in the Body's use of the *Rules* following a meeting in the context of an actual decision.[28]

+ A copy (possibly laminated) of the Summary of Rules and the Matrix of Points and Motions found at the end of this handbook at Appendices B and C can be permanently placed at each position of the dais for the Members' ease of reference.

CHAPTER 2

TERMINOLOGY

Some words and phrases used in *Bob's Rules of Order* convey a specific meaning when referring to a practice, an action, or a person involved in a meeting. The *Rules* capitalize some of these words and phrases (e.g., "Body," "Presiding Officer," "Member," and "Floor") to remind the reader that the word or phrase holds a specifically defined meaning.

Agenda Item

An issue, topic, matter, case, application, or other subject to be addressed by the Body during a meeting. An agenda item includes items initially listed on the meeting agenda as well as items later added to the meeting agenda in accordance with the Body's bylaws or other meeting policy or practice.

Amendment (or to Amend)

An action to change, to add words to, or to omit words from a debatable motion on the Floor. The amendment is usually intended to clarify or improve the wording of the original motion.

Body

The council, board, commission, or other formally constituted organization that adopted these rules of order to govern the organization's meetings.

Debatable Motion

A motion that is subject to debate by the Body in accordance with the rules of order. The debatable motions are the Principal Motion, Continue or Postpone, Amend, Reconsider, and Adjourn.

Floor

✦ As to a Member or a person participating in the meeting, a recognition that the Member or person was granted the exclusive right to address the Body.

✦ As to a motion, a recognition that a motion was properly stated and received a second in accordance with these rules of order and is properly before the Body for consideration.

Member

A person elected or appointed to hold office or a position with the Body and who is authorized to participate and to vote on a motion pending before the Body. The term Member also includes (i) the Presiding Officer and (ii) a person serving as an alternate or other ancillary or subordinate position on the Body when the person is authorized to both actively participate in the consideration of a matter before the Body and to vote on a motion.

Motion

A formal proposal seeking a specific action by the Body that is typically preceded by the words "I move that ..." or "I make a motion that ...." Motions are generally introduced by voice but may be presented to the Body in writing.

Moving Member

The Member offering a motion or a point to the Body for consideration and action.

Objection

A verbal declaration by a Member in the form of "objection," "I object," or other similar words offered for the purpose of declaring to the Body that the offer of a So Moved Motion, a Friendly Withdrawal, or a Friendly Amendment is not acceptable to the Member.

Out of Order

An action or a failure to act in accordance with the rules of order.

Open

To formally announce or introduce an agenda item to the Body, which would allow the Body to initiate consideration of the agenda item.

Point

A verbal declaration by a Member addressed to the Presiding Officer requesting to bring before the Body a matter for immediate decision or resolution. There are three recognized points: (1) Point of Order, (2) Point of Information, and (3) Point of Appeal.

Presiding Officer

The person elected, appointed, or selected to preside over the meeting of the Body. The Presiding Officer will customarily be the mayor or chairperson of the Body but may include an officer designated in advance by the Body to preside over the meeting upon the absence of the mayor or chairperson, such as the mayor pro tem or vice chairperson. The Body's bylaws may also assign the role of Presiding Officer in the absence of the mayor/mayor pro tem or the chairperson/vice chairperson.

Quorum

The minimal number of Members required to be present and eligible to act in order to conduct business on behalf of the Body.

Second

A verbal declaration by a Member in the form of "second," "I second," or other similar words. A proper second clearly expresses the Member's support that a motion offered to the Body by a Moving Member should receive debate.

Withdraw

To remove a motion from the Floor, effectively and permanently terminating all consideration of the motion by the Body.

Special Terminology

Legislative, Quasi-Judicial, and Administrative Powers

The governing bodies of Colorado local governments may exercise three different powers when making decisions in the conduct of government business: legislative power, quasi-judicial power, and administrative power. Many of the government's boards and commissions may also exercise one or more of these powers. For example, the planning and zoning commission or the board of adjustment will often exercise quasi-judicial power when considering the approval of landowners' applications yet also provide recommendations to the governing body on matters that are legislative or administrative in nature.

It is necessary to understand the basic differences between these three different powers. Meeting procedures may vary depending on which power is exercised. Moreover, *Bob's Rules of Order* references these different powers in the application of the procedural rules.

Legislative Power or Decision

Legislative power or legislative decisions customarily involve the consideration and adoption of laws or policies that will affect the interests of the general public and may affect specific persons only in the abstract.[29] Legislative actions involve the exercise of significant discretion by the decision-making Body. Because legislative power involves the making of laws or policies, this power is commonly reserved to the elected governing body (e.g., the city council, board of trustees, or board of county commissioners). Some advisory boards and commissions may aid the governing body by offering recommendations on legislative matters, and, in this context, the actions by the advisory board or commission are also legislative in nature, although these bodies do not reach final decisions or enact legislation.

Quasi-Judicial Power or Decision

Quasi-judicial[30] power or quasi-judicial decisions involve the application of the law to facts that are established during a hearing and the rendering of a decision that affects the interests of specific individuals.[31] Quasi-judicial actions most often include the submission of an application to the government, a requirement that the government issue public notice for a hearing at which interested parties are entitled to be heard, and a requirement that the government timely render a final decision on the application concerning the applicant's legal rights. Many types of zoning and land-use matters and some licensing decisions (e.g., issuance of a new liquor license) involve the exercise of quasi-judicial power.

Administrative (or Executive) Power or Decision

Administrative power or administrative decisions involve the implementation or execution of the laws and policies enacted by the legislative Body of the local government. Administrative power does not establish new legislative law or policy, and the power relates to matters that are typically temporary in operation or effect.[32] The power is commonly exercised by the chief executive or administrative officer (e.g., manager or administrator and the administrative staff). However, the governing body and other bodies of the government will from time to time engage in administrative action, such as deciding future agenda items for a meeting or directing staff to pursue a certain course of action in the management of the government's affairs.

"Discussion" and "Debate"

Virtually all organized bodies use an agenda to manage the business of a public meeting. Local governments are no different. The local government's agenda is typically comprised of a list of individual agenda items. The process for scheduling items for an agenda may be formally described in the Body's bylaws or may be a product of long-standing and informal administrative practice.

Each agenda item presents a topic, issue, hearing, or other business matter to be considered and, if needed, decided by the Body. The typical individual agenda item proceeds through a series of steps: (1) the item is officially opened for the Body's consideration; (2) information is presented to the Body; (3) the item is considered by the Body; and (4) the Body takes an action to decide, continue, or otherwise conclude the agenda item. The Body repeats this general process for each agenda item until the business on the agenda is addressed and the meeting is adjourned.

Understanding the local government's typical steps for the processing of an agenda item helps clarify the use of the terms "discussion" and "debate" in *Bob's Rules of Order* and the relationship of these two different actions to a motion.

In short, the term "discussion" is used for the Body's action prior to a motion; the term "debate" is used for the Body's action after the motion.

"Discussion" means "the act of exchanging views on something"[33] or "the instance of discussing; consideration or examination ... especially to explore solutions."[34] In local government, the discussion step before a motion typically focuses the Body's attention on a problem, an issue, or a topic. Members offer perspectives and viewpoints on the matter, suggest that the Body explore potential solutions, and ask questions to collect the information needed to decide a possible course of action. The broader nature of the word "discuss" suits the practice commonly undertaken by local government bodies prior to the presentation of a motion.

In contrast, "debate" means "a formal contest in which the affirmative and negative sides of a proposition are advocated by opposing speakers."[35] A common dictionary recognizes that "debate" in the context of government means a "formal discussion of a motion before a deliberative body according to the rules of parliamentary procedure."[36] Debate is a term well suited to describe the process that local government undertakes after a motion is proposed that expresses a proposition for the Body's consideration and possible action. As a very general graphic illustration of the proper use of "discussion" and "debate" in the context of *Bob's Rules*, the following illustration may prove helpful:

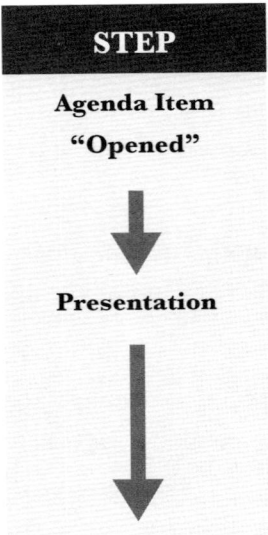

STEP	ACTION INVOLVED
Agenda Item "Opened"	An initial announcement to the Body by a staff member, clerk, or the Presiding Officer of the agenda item.
Presentation	Information relevant to the agenda item is presented. In a quasi-judicial hearing, this step involves a formal presentation to the Body of testimony and evidence from staff, the applicant, and interested citizens.

Discussion

The Body asks questions and discusses the information provided during the presentation. Discussion may frame the issues to be resolved or decided. For a quasi-judicial matter, the Body may be advised to limit discussion to the clarification of the evidence and testimony and to withhold Members' opinions on whether the quasi-judicial matter should be approved or rejected.

Motion

Armed with the information from the presentation and the discussion steps, a motion is offered to the Body by a Member.

Debate

The Body engages in debate regarding the proposition presented by the motion. Members deliberate and express support or opposition to the motion. Debate may result in amendment, continuation or postponement, withdrawal, or a vote on the motion.

Vote

A vote is taken on the motion. If the motion fails, the Body may return to discussion and a potential new motion or may move to the next agenda item.

"Continue" and "Postpone"

The terms "continue" and "postpone" are used in local government meetings interchangeably even though they do not necessarily share the same meaning.[37] Because the interchangeable use of the terms is now ingrained in common meeting practice, *Bob's Rules of Order* recognizes this common practice in the context of a motion to delay the consideration of an agenda item to a future date, to an uncertain date, or indefinitely. See Section 16.0, Motion to Continue or Postpone.

"Abstain" and "Recuse"

Bob's Rules of Order recognizes a difference between a Member abstaining from a vote and a Member's recusal from a vote.

"Abstaining" means to "not vote for or against something."[38] In contrast, "recusal" means "to remove oneself as a judge or policymaker in a particular matter, [especially] because of a conflict of interest."[39]

In keeping with the common and clear meaning of these terms and in the application of *Bob's Rules*, a Member will "abstain" when the Member does not cast a "yes" or "no" vote on a matter and there is no legal impediment preventing the Member from voting.[40] Where a Member is legally precluded from voting on a matter—when the Member has a conflict of interest, for example—the Member will "recuse" themselves from participation and the vote.

CHAPTER 3

THE RULES

Bob's Rules of Order establishes rules governing the various aspects of a public meeting. The rules are set forth in the following order:

1.0   The Meeting Generally

2.0   The Quorum

3.0   The Presiding Officer

4.0   The Floor

5.0   The Motion

6.0   The Friendly Requests

7.0   The Vote

8.0   Rule Suspension and Rule Deviation

1.0   The Meeting Generally

Rule 1.1

Any state or local law that concerns the conduct of a meeting is a part of the *Rules of Order* to the extent the law is applicable to the Body.

Commentary

A decision of the Body is not final and defensible solely because the meeting and the decision-making process complied with the *Rules of Order*. Meetings are also governed by requirements imposed by the Body's bylaws and other local governing policies, as well as state law, such as the Colorado Open Meetings Law.

Compliance with all applicable state and local meeting laws and policies, together with *Bob's Rules of Order*, is made a requirement of a meeting by Rule 1.1. The rule effectively authorizes the Members to use a Point of Order to bring the Body into compliance with all applicable meeting laws in addition to the *Rules of Order*.

Rule 1.2

The meeting agenda will be followed unless properly amended or modified.

Commentary

An efficient meeting is, in part, the result of organization. Organization is best achieved by following a meeting agenda. To promote organization and efficiency, Rule 1.2 requires that the meeting agenda be followed and that the agenda items be addressed in the order presented.

Rule 1.2 must necessarily recognize that an agenda may require amendment or modification. A Motion to Continue or Postpone is one circumstance through which the agenda may be modified and items on the agenda moved to a future date and time or postponed indefinitely. Moreover, a Principal Motion[41] can be proposed to formally amend the agenda to reorder agenda items as the Body deems appropriate. The Presiding Officer also holds the discretion pursuant to Rule 3.4 to change the agenda. The Presiding Officer's decision to change an agenda is subject to a Point of Order or a Point of Appeal. See Section 11.0 (Point of Order) and Section 13.0 (Point of Appeal).

Importantly, the Body should use caution when adding items to the agenda. Obviously, matters that require advance notice to the public cannot be added to an agenda.[42] The local government's charter or ordinances may also impose advance public notice requirements for certain matters, which may preclude a last-minute addition to an agenda. Moreover, the Colorado Open Meetings Law expresses the public policy that the public notice of the local government meeting includes "specific agenda information where possible."[43] However, executive sessions need not be noted in advance on an agenda and may be added at any time, even during a meeting, provided that the motion for executive session receives the required supermajority vote. See Section 22.0.

Rule 1.3

The Body may presume that any legally required public notice for the meeting and for each agenda item was properly completed.

Commentary

Full and timely notice to the public is required for any meeting[44] "at which the adoption of any proposed policy, position, resolution, rule, regulation, or formal action occurs or at which a majority or quorum of the body is in attendance or is expected to be in attendance."[45]

Rule 1.3 does not specify the form of the notice for a meeting (i.e., the content or the manner of publication of the notice). The form of notice for the meeting must comport with state and local law.[46]

Very importantly, individual agenda items considered during a properly noticed meeting may also require a separate notice or multiple notices[47] that may vary from the general notice for the meeting.[48] The Body is strongly encouraged to consult with the Body's local legal counsel or an experienced local government administrative clerk concerning the required form of public notice.

In the interest of meeting efficiency, Rule 1.3 authorizes the Body to presume that the legally required notice was properly completed for the meeting generally and, when required, was properly completed for each agenda item. This presumption is reasonable because the issuance of public notices for a meeting is a practice both known to and routinely undertaken by the administrative staff in setting the meeting and in supporting the Body's decision-making process.

This Rule 1.3 presumption permits the Body to forego the need to take the time to determine or to announce during the meeting that notice was properly completed before convening the meeting or opening an agenda item. However, this rule does not prevent the Body from following a practice of confirming that notice was issued for the meeting generally or issued for any specific agenda item. In addition, the rule does not preclude a Member from questioning whether proper notice was provided for the meeting.

The presumption that notice was properly completed is rebuttable, meaning that issuance of proper notice shall be a presumed fact of the meeting and the agenda item until such time that credible evidence is provided to disprove the fact.

Rule 1.4

A Member shall disclose a conflict of interest and recuse themselves from both participation and voting when required by applicable state or local law.

Commentary

It is not uncommon that a Member will encounter a conflict of interest that is recognized by state or local law prior to or during a meeting.

State law provides for a number of different circumstances in which a Member may be conflicted and could be required to not participate and to not vote on a matter before the Body.[49] Charters, ordinances, local bylaws, and local codes of ethics may also establish circumstances that give rise to a conflict of interest. *Bob's Rules* does not specify when a conflict of interest may exist. The existence of a conflict, and the proper means to address a conflict, involves analysis of statutory provisions, judicial interpretations, and local laws. The Body's attorney should be consulted concerning potential conflicts of interest, and this consultation is often imperative to protect the integrity of the Body's decision-making process.

Rule 1.4 requires a Member's recusal[50] regardless of when the conflict is found to exist. A conflict of interest known to the Member prior to the opening of the agenda item should result in the conflicted Member recusing themselves prior to the Body opening the item for consideration. A conflict realized during an agenda item may require recusal immediately upon the discovery of the conflict.

A conflict will often require the Member to disclose to the Body the general nature giving rise to the conflict of interest. Upon this disclosure, the Member should request that the Presiding Officer recuse the Member from the agenda item, and the Presiding Officer should grant the request when the recusal is justified. A conflict of interest held by the Presiding Officer should likewise be disclosed, and the recusal should immediately be followed by the Presiding Officer's relinquishment of the chair to the person assigned the role of leadership in the absence of the Presiding Officer. Upon recusal, the conflicted Member or conflicted Presiding Officer should depart the dais. The Body's legal counsel may also suggest that the Member or Presiding Officer also temporarily depart the meeting room during the consideration of the agenda item—or the Body's bylaws may require such departure—to avoid concerns that the conflicted person may influence the process through facial expression or body language. Again, the Body's legal counsel should directly aid the Body and the conflicted Member in properly addressing a conflict of interest.

Rule 1.5

A motion is not required for the Body to initiate discussion.

Commentary

Some meeting rules of order[51] and a few local governmental bodies follow a rule that both a motion and a second are prerequisites to the undertaking of any substantive discussion on any matter. However, such a rule is inconsistent with the needs and practices of the common local government meeting.

It is exceedingly common that an agenda item is introduced and the Floor opened for discussion without a motion. Substantive discussion will also follow informational reports and updates that do not require a motion or a decision from the Body. And, in many instances, the specific question to be answered or decision to be made is not known to the Body upon the introduction of the agenda item.

Allowing discussion before a motion and debate allows the Body to receive information and discuss possible options for action. This discussion is often helpful in the framing of a motion. Requiring a motion to be on the Floor before the Body may engage in any conversation may focus or limit the Body's attention on the motion's singular or specific proposition or request for action. Moreover, any motion that precedes substantive discussion may need to be withdrawn or amended to address the issues raised in the Body's debate on the motion.

For quasi-judicial matters, it may appear inconsistent with the requirements of due process and fairness to present a motion to approve or deny an application prior to the receipt of any information, evidence, or testimony.[52] An early motion may create an appearance to the public that the Moving Member has prejudged the application based on information received prior to the meeting or only upon the information assembled in the Body's meeting packet.

Nevertheless, Rule 1.5 allows, but does not mandate, discussion before the presentation of a motion. Requiring a motion before discussion is a practice that is ingrained in the meeting procedures for some local government bodies and may stem from a longstanding adherence to *Robert's Rules of Order*. Such practice may continue under Rule 1.5. A motion may be offered at the proper time, which may be before, during, or following the discussion on an agenda item.

Special Note: Discussion of Quasi-Judicial Matters

Members sitting as judges for a quasi-judicial matter must remain fair, impartial, and unbiased and judge the matter based only on the record developed before the Body.[53]

During the discussion period and prior to a motion, the Body will receive evidence from the applicant seeking approval of an application, from the administrative staff, and from persons who support or oppose the application. To best ensure fairness and impartiality, Members should refrain from offering opinions regarding their support or disapproval of the application prior to the presentation of all the evidence. Such opinions prior to the receipt of all the evidence may reveal a bias or a prejudgment of the quasi-judicial matter. Additionally, Members should remain acutely aware that the form or the manner of questions asked during discussion may reveal a bias or a pre-decision. All comments and questions during discussion should remain free of judgement or opinion on the matter.

Following the full presentation of the information and evidence, and following a motion, the Body may engage in debate and deliberation on the motion's proposal. The Members may then offer their opinions on whether the testimony and evidence support or fail to support the standards and criteria governing the decision on the quasi-judicial application.

Rule 1.6

The record for each decision of the Body includes all information presented to the Body that pertains to the decision, all discussion and debate of the Body in reaching the decision, and all laws and local policies applicable to the decision.

Commentary

Every decision will be based on information presented to the Body. The information supplied to the Body may be in the form of a staff report and supporting documents, letters, emails, plans, drawings, photographs, presentations by applicants and staff, opinions from experts and consultants, testimony and comments from citizens, and answers to questions posed by the Body. For legislative or administrative matters only, the Members may also offer their own experiences or knowledge that is relevant to the decision.

Lastly, the relevant or applicable laws and local policies that will guide the decision are part of the information available to the Body.

Rule 1.6 confirms that all information presented during the meeting will create the record for the Body's ultimate decision. Rule 1.6 allows the Body to forgo the need to acknowledge each item that would be part of the record in a matter and to forgo the need to "read into the record" the titles of documents or reports available to the Body.

Special Note: Member Testimony on Quasi-Judicial Matters

Because Members sit as judges for a quasi-judicial matter, they are not witnesses, meaning it is not the role of the Members to testify as to facts underlying the matter to be decided. As judges, Members are to evaluate the factual information presented by others during a quasi-judicial hearing, and they do not serve as the *source* of the information to be evaluated.[54] Caution should always be exercised by a Member in a quasi-judicial setting to refrain from serving as a witness.

Rule 1.7

The Body's decision on a matter is presumed to be supported by the record and by reasonable inferences drawn from the record.

Commentary

Every Member is encouraged to offer their individual evaluation of the information contained in the record and to identify how the record supports the Member's vote. This practice may be critically important for quasi-judicial matters where the Body must determine whether the record supports the relevant criteria for approval of the quasi-judicial application.

But, even when the Members explain how the record supports their vote, it is unlikely that the Members will identify *all* of the information in the record that may support their vote. It is also unfortunately common that some Members remain silent prior to casting a vote because they believe that the basis for their vote is apparent from the record. To address these concerns, Rule 1.7 enables the Body to support its decision based upon the entirety of the record, notwithstanding incomplete explanations by the Members or even the silence of some Members.

Rule 1.7 promotes meeting efficiency. It would significantly delay a meeting, or require the continuation of a meeting, to allow the time for the Body to comprehensively review the details of the record and to exhaust all the possible reasons supporting a decision. Rule 1.7 allows the Body to rely upon the entire record, and upon the reasonable inferences that can be found in the record, when justifying the Body's decision.

Importantly, Members should not use Rule 1.7 as an excuse or a justification to forgo the offer of opinions, explanations, and reasoning during debate that will support their vote. Notwithstanding Rule 1.7, the Member's opinions and explanations will always form the primary and best evidence when defending the Body's decisions.

Special Note: Quasi-Judicial Findings

In a quasi-judicial matter, the Body's decision must be supported by information found in the record; otherwise, the decision may be subject to challenge as arbitrary or capricious.[55] The value of the record is highlighted by the fact that a court will limit its review to only the record created during the Body's consideration of the quasi-judicial matter. The record is critically important.

The record will oftentimes include a staff report, a staff recommendation for approval or denial, and documents and testimony by the applicant and others supporting a certain outcome. Where the record clearly supports the Body's ultimate decision, any challenge of the Body's decision may prove unsuccessful.

However, when a Member disagrees with the information and recommendations contained in the record that support a specific outcome, it is important that the disagreeing Member explain during debate why the information in the record supports a contrary conclusion. Without such an explanation, there may be an insufficient basis to justify a contrary vote and a contrary decision by the Body. Although Rule 1.7 may enable the Body to rely upon the entire record and reasonable inferences drawn from the record to support a decision, where the record may not clearly support a Member's contrary position or vote, the disagreeing Member must "speak up" during debate and deliberation on the motion.

Rule 1.8

A meeting formally ends only upon the Presiding Officer's declaration of adjournment without objection or upon the approval of a Motion to Adjourn.

Commentary

Every meeting must end. Rule 1.8 recognizes that the point in time for the end of the meeting requires an official and affirmative announcement or action. Otherwise, Members may casually leave the dais or exit the meeting room, which would put into doubt whether the meeting ended or whether the meeting may reconvene later.

A meeting of the Body will end only upon the Presiding Officer's formal declaration of adjournment pursuant to Rule 3.4 without objection from a Member. Alternatively, the meeting will end upon approval of a Motion to Adjourn pursuant to Section 21.0.

2.0   The Quorum

Rule 2.1

A quorum of the Body is required for the Body to conduct business unless otherwise expressly provided by the Body's bylaws or the *Rules of Order*.

Commentary

An important tenet for any Body is that business is conducted, and decisions are made, only in the presence of a sufficient number of members to represent the Body. The minimum number of members needed to represent the Body and conduct business is called the "quorum." The required quorum should be determined for each type of meeting by the Body's bylaws or other policy.[56]

In accordance with Rule 2.1, business cannot be conducted, and decisions made, in the absence of the required quorum for the meeting. An important and necessary exception to Rule 2.1 is recognized by Rule 2.5, which authorizes limited action and decisions in the absence of a quorum.

Rule 2.1 accommodates the situation where a quorum fails to attend a properly scheduled and noticed meeting yet the Members in attendance desire to informally discuss general—but not quasi-judicial[57]—matters. In this situation, the Colorado Open Meetings Law authorizes informal discussion of public business with less than a quorum in attendance provided that the meeting is open to the public.[58] The lack of a quorum, however, prohibits those Members attending the meeting from making any decisions or conducting any business in accordance with Rule 2.1.

Rule 2.2

Unless otherwise provided by the Body's bylaws or other applicable law, a majority of the total membership of the Body who are present and eligible to vote shall constitute a quorum.

Commentary

The Body's bylaws or other governing policy will commonly establish a quorum requirement for the Body's meetings. Rule 2.2 defers to the quorum standards set by the Body.

However, Rule 2.2 sets a default standard for the determination of a quorum where no other law, policy, or rule requires a different standard. If the Body has not set a quorum standard for the meeting, Rule 2.2 will prevent a minority of the members of the Body from conducting business.

For the purpose of Rule 2.2, the phrase "total membership" means the total number of authorized voting positions for the Body.[59] The Body's total membership is a fixed number that will not vary due to Member vacancies or absences.

When determining whether a Member is to be included in the determination of a quorum, the phrase "present and eligible to vote" recognizes that the quorum determination must exclude Members who are absent from the meeting or who are ineligible to vote due to a conflict of interest.

The determination that a quorum exists is an ongoing process which may change during the course of a meeting. For example, at the initial commencement of a meeting and prior to conducting any business, the quorum required will be determined from those Members who are present[60] and who are eligible voting members of the Body.[61]

Following the commencement of the meeting with the required quorum, the quorum may change due to a Member's absence from the meeting or a Member's ineligibility to participate due to a conflict of interest. Where a change in the number of Members present and eligible to vote reduces the quorum below the minimum quorum requirement, the Body will be unable to conduct business and make decisions. In such cases, postponement of the meeting's agenda items will be necessary in accordance with Rule 2.5. Additionally, the quorum determination may involve Rules 2.3 and 2.4, which address the effect on the quorum for excused and unexcused absences arising during the consideration of a motion.

Rule 2.3

A request to be excused from the meeting while a motion is on the Floor, if granted, shall be effective:

✦ **Upon the granting of the request if the excuse is due to a lawfully recognized conflict of interest; or**

✦ **Upon the granting of the request if the excused Member's absence will not deny the Body of a quorum; or**

✦ **Upon the final vote or other final resolution of the pending motion if the excused Member's absence will deny the Body of a quorum.**

Commentary

A Member's request to be excused during a meeting is not uncommon. A request may be due to a conflict of interest, illness, or an unforeseen emergency. When the excuse is justified in accordance with the Body's bylaws, the request should customarily be accommodated. [62]

An excused absence during a meeting may impact the established quorum. [63] A justified request to be excused made between the consideration of agenda items or when no motion is on the Floor enables the Presiding Officer to grant the request and permit the excuse to be immediately effective. The Body can then address any potential impact on the existing quorum and the Body's ability to conduct business. See Rule 2.5.

However, a request to be excused from the meeting while a motion is on the Floor and under debate may potentially be attributed to a Member seeking to deny the Body the quorum necessary to render a decision. Rule 2.3 seeks to balance a Member's justifiable need to be excused from attendance with the Body's need to maintain the quorum to resolve a pending motion. To best strike this balance, an excuse granted during a meeting while a motion is on the Floor will be effective as provided by Rule 2.3.

Rule 2.3 does not preclude a quorum of the Body from entertaining a Motion to Continue or Postpone the motion on the Floor in accordance with Section 16.0. Moreover, if the request to be excused is not granted by the Presiding Officer and the requesting Member leaves the meeting, Rule 2.4 will be applicable.

Rule 2.4

A Member's *unexcused* absence while a motion is on the Floor shall not affect the quorum until the final vote or other final resolution of the motion.

Commentary

On occasion, a Member may leave the meeting after the required quorum was established. When the departure from the meeting is *unexcused*, the absence is problematic. Absences can effectively make it more challenging to obtain a decisive vote on a pending motion.[64] Perhaps of equal importance, a Member's absence will deny citizens of their voice in a pending public matter that they expect to be expressed by their elected or appointed representative.

The more significant problem with a Member's unexcused absence arises from an absence during the consideration of a motion on the Floor. An unexcused absence by a Member during debate on a motion will oftentimes be attributed to the Member attempting to intentionally undermine the quorum and the Body's ability to act on a pending motion. In fact, some local governments have unfortunately encountered this problem. A rule designed to address an unexcused and unjustified absence and its resulting impact upon a pending motion is necessary to ensure that the Body can maintain the quorum and address the immediate needs of the public pending before the Body.

Rule 2.4 requires the Body to consider a Member who departs a meeting without excuse while a motion is on the Floor as remaining present for purposes of resolving the pending motion. This approach is reasonable given that the absence is entirely voluntary by the Member. An unexcused absence is equivalent to the Member staying seated on the dais and refusing to participate in the debate or to vote on the pending motion. The Member's effective refusal to vote "yes" or "no" is addressed by Rule 7.5.

Rule 2.5

In the absence of a quorum, the Presiding Officer, the Members present, or an administrative staff member shall:

+ **Postpone all unresolved agenda items to the next regular meeting; and**

+ **Adjourn the meeting.**

Commentary

The Body may confront the absence of a quorum either at the outset of the meeting or later in a meeting that was commenced with a required quorum. When the absence of a quorum cannot be resolved by a delay to await the attendance of the Members who comprise a quorum, it will be necessary to address any unresolved agenda items.

As provided by Rule 2.1, less than a quorum of the body cannot conduct business or make a decision. Rule 2.5 supports an exception to this rule by expressly authorizing limited action to address the Body's inability to conduct business due to the lack of a quorum.

The most crucial step in the absence of a quorum is to address *quasi-judicial* matters on the agenda. For quasi-judicial matters, the applicant, interested parties, and the public received formal notice of the date, time, and place of the quasi-judicial hearing. It is necessary to postpone quasi-judicial matters formally and publicly prior to the adjournment of the meeting as a matter of fairness to everyone seeking to attend or participate in the hearing.[65]

Additionally, the lack of a quorum can create confusion concerning the status of any items listed on the agenda. Obviously, the absence of a quorum cannot form a decision, a vote, or a directive of the Body to remove the unresolved agenda items from any future consideration by the Body. A rule that addresses the status of unresolved agenda items in the case of the lack of a quorum is necessary to avoid confusion and uncertainty.

Rule 2.5 requires certain members present at the meeting to manage the agenda in the absence of a quorum. By way of hierarchy, the Presiding Officer is required by Rule 2.5 to take action; in the absence of a Presiding Officer, one or more of the Members are required to take action; and, in the absence of any Members, an administrative staff member (oftentimes the Body's clerk) shall take action. The action is simple. An announcement of the postponement of all unresolved agenda items to the next regular meeting is in order. The announcement should include information that will clearly apprise the public and other interested parties of the date, time, and place of the postponed meeting.

For example, to address the lack of a quorum necessary to begin a meeting, the necessary announcement might say:

"Due to the lack of a quorum for our June 1, 2026, scheduled meeting, all matters on the agenda are postponed until the next meeting of the Body, which will be held on April 6, 2026, beginning at 6:00 p.m. here in the City Council Chambers, 123 Main Street."

To address an absence of a quorum arising during a meeting that was initially started with the necessary quorum, the announcement might say:

"Due to the current lack of a quorum, the remaining items on the agenda, which are items 6(b) through 9(c), are postponed until the next meeting of the Body, which will be held on April 6, 2026, beginning at 5:30 p.m. here in the Town Meeting Hall, 601 First Avenue."

Importantly, Rule 2.5 does not preclude the Body from calling a special meeting in accordance with the Body's bylaws and requirements for notice in order to address matters postponed due to the lack of a quorum.

3.0 The Presiding Officer

Rule 3.1
The Presiding Officer shall be the exclusive director and facilitator of all meeting conduct.

Commentary

The Body's efficiency and effectiveness is dependent upon the formal recognition of one Member to administer the meeting agenda, manage discussion and debate, oversee Members' fair access to the Floor, and render decisions on meeting procedure. For all local government bodies, there is customarily one person elected, appointed, or otherwise designated to serve as the Presiding Officer for a meeting. Rule 3.1 formally confers authority for meeting direction and facilitation to the designated Presiding Officer.

Rule 3.2

The Presiding Officer serves as the parliamentarian unless the role is assigned to another person.

Commentary

The need to decide a question concerning the proper application of the *Rules* will invariably arise during a meeting. Most commonly, the question will be whether a particular motion is or is not out of order. The term "parliamentarian" describes the person with a sound understanding of the *Rules* and who decides questions about the proper application of a rule.

For many local government bodies, the Presiding Officer acts as the parliamentarian without any formal assignment of the role. When the role is expressly assigned, however, it is often assigned to the Presiding Officer. This assignment can help advance meeting efficiency given that the Presiding Officer leads the meeting, may exercise discretion concerning meeting procedure, and has direct access to the Floor during the meeting without a need for a formal request.

Some local governmental bodies assign the role of parliamentarian to the Body's secretary, an administrative clerk or staff person, or the Body's legal counsel. Such an assignment may prove efficient where the person assigned the role has a sound knowledge and experience in the application of the *Rules*, can quickly make decisions without delaying the flow of the meeting, can be diplomatic and professional when offering advice and direction during a meeting, and has the Members' confidence to serve as a fair and impartial parliamentarian.

Members may use a Point of Appeal to challenge the parliamentarian's decision. See Section 13.0. Moreover, the Presiding Officer or the assigned parliamentarian is always encouraged to consult with the Body's legal counsel or administrative staff to help make decisions regarding the proper application of the *Rules of Order*.

Rule 3.3

The Presiding Officer is entitled to the same rights as a Member unless otherwise limited by law.

Commentary

The Presiding Officer's role as the facilitator or director of the meeting should not limit the Presiding Officer's role or responsibly as a Member of the Body. The Presiding Officer may hold an opinion, join in discussion, offer a motion, second a motion, engage in debate,[66] and, when legally authorized, vote. The Presiding Officer is a full Member of the Body.

Very importantly, the *Rules of Order* recognizes that, in some instances, state or local law limits or restricts the Presiding Officer's powers. For example, the mayor in a statutory town is the Presiding Officer of meetings,[67] and, by local ordinance, the governing body may deny the mayor the right to vote except in the event of a tie vote among the other Members.[68] The Presiding Officer should consult with the

Body's legal counsel to understand any limitations or restrictions on the Presiding Officer's powers as a Member of the Body. Compliance with state or local law regarding meetings can be enforced through a Point of Order. See Rule 1.1 and Section 11.0.

Rule 3.4

The Presiding Officer may exercise discretion during the meeting subject to a Point of Order or a Point of Appeal.

Commentary

The Presiding Officer must conduct meetings and follow the *Rules of Order*. However, the *Rules of Order* expressly recognizes that meeting efficiency may, at times, be advanced by a temporary deviation from a rule. A deviation from strict compliance with a rule is common, and Members rarely raise an objection to a deviation when the deviation will advance meeting efficiency. Given that deviations from a Body's adopted rules of order are common and accepted, Rule 3.4 is necessary.

In the application of the *Rules* during a meeting, some examples of opportunities for the exercise of discretion include:

+ Adjourning the meeting or calling for a recess without a formal motion and vote.

+ Calling for the vote on a motion, which will effectively close the potential for continuing debate on a motion.

+ Declaring a Friendly Amendment or Friendly Withdrawal of a motion without a request from a Member.

+ Calling a Member to order without a Point of Order.

✦ Asking for information without a Point of Information.

✦ Taking agenda items out of order when, for example, the necessary persons are not yet in attendance.

✦ Electing not to call the Body to order when an immaterial deviation from a rule occurs.

✦ Suspending a rule as authorized by Rule 8.1.

One common and appropriate exercise of discretion is forgoing a formal motion as required by Rule 5.1 when the action proposed is administrative, ministerial, and minor in nature. Such action may include, by way of examples, directing the administrative staff to prepare a report for the Body's later consideration, making a simple revision to the minutes prior to formal approval, or directing the postponement of the scheduled closure of the local swimming pool until a specific date. For these administrative matters, the Body may direct the action at the request of the Presiding Officer by expressing the Body's general concurrence or consent.[69] Importantly, forgoing a formal motion and vote should not be used for legislative or quasi-judicial decisions. Such decisions are not ministerial or minor in nature and often require a formal recording of the Body's vote on a specific proposition.

In some limited circumstances, the local home rule charter, ordinance, or policy may provide that the Body may only act by ordinance, resolution, or motion. These types of provisions could be interpreted as prohibiting the use of an informal consensus by the Body even for minor matters. The Body's legal counsel should be consulted in deciding the proper interpretation of any charter, ordinance, or other policy provisions that may limit the authority to forgo a motion and render decisions informally.

At all times, a discretionary decision by the Presiding Officer remains subject to a Point of Order and Point of Appeal, which allows the Members to bring the meeting into compliance with the *Rules of Order*.

Rule 3.5

The Presiding Officer shall facilitate the meeting in a fair and neutral manner and, whenever practicable, defer to the Members to initially lead discussion, offer motions, and direct debate.

Commentary

Rules 3.1, 3.2, and 8.1 empower the Presiding Officer to exclusively direct meeting conduct and exercise discretion regarding meeting procedures. Rule 3.3 also affords the Presiding Officer the same rights as Members to hold and express an opinion or position as to matters before the Body and to offer and second motions. However, when the Presiding Officer holds an opinion or a desire for a particular outcome, the Presiding Officer's power over the conduct of the meeting could be exercised in a manner that impinges or impairs the rights of the Members.

Rule 3.5 directs the Presiding Offer to conduct the meeting in a fair and neutral manner. The Presiding Officer should defer to the Members to initially propose motions and to lead discussion and debate. This deference is a reasonable means of ensuring fairness and protecting the Members' rights. Following an offer to the Members for the first opportunity to provide input, the Presiding Officer is entitled to exercise the right to express opinions and to participate in discussion and debate in accordance with Rule 3.3. The Presiding Officer may also offer or second a motion when the Members sit silent after the Presiding Officer extends the first opportunity to the Members to participate.

At times, the Presiding Officer may be unable to facilitate a meeting in a fair and neutral manner due to the Presiding Officer's strong, passionate, or biased position regarding a matter pending before the Body. The discretion afforded the Presiding Officer by Rule 3.4 authorizes the Presiding Officer to "pass the gavel" and hand off the facilitation of the meeting to another Member. Once no longer seated as the Presiding Officer, full participation in the meeting without the limitation imposed on the Presiding Officer by Rules 3.1 and 3.5 is then allowed.[70]

4.0 The Floor

Rule 4.1
The Floor is required to address the Body.

Commentary

A rule requiring a Member to obtain the Floor in order to speak to the Body is universally recognized as a principal element of an efficient and orderly meeting.

The wisdom of Rule 4.1 is sound. If Members were unrestricted in their ability to speak during a meeting, then, in the worst-case scenario, Members would continuously talk over and interrupt one another, with the more assertive or aggressive Members raising their voices to be heard. In the best-case scenario, Members would self-police their access to the Floor in a courteous manner in support of the goal of fairness and equality among all Members. It goes without saying that something akin to the worst case is unfortunately too common due to the vagaries of personalities in any group of people who are passionate about issues. A rule is therefore necessary to curtail unrestricted access to the Floor for the sake of meeting efficiency.

Rule 4.1 does not preclude a Member's interruption of another Member who has the Floor to offer a Point of Order, a Point of Information, or a Point of Appeal. All points are privileged. See Rule 10.1. A Member may express a point to the Body without first requesting permission to obtain the Floor. See Rule 10.2. Nevertheless, Members should offer a point in a courteous fashion and await a break in the discussion or debate.

A corollary to this rule is that Members may not hold conversations "on the side" with each other or with administrative staff during a meeting. Such conversations may not only interfere with the discussion or debate but may also impair the other participants' ability to hear and may also interfere with the recording of the meeting.

Rule 4.2

A Member shall be granted the Floor by the Presiding Officer when properly requested in accordance with the *Rules of Order* and local meeting practice.

Commentary

One of the most important goals for a meeting is to protect each Member's right to be heard during discussion and debate.

Rules 4.1 and 4.4, together with the nature of representative government and fairness, necessarily *infer* that a Member will not be denied reasonable access to the Floor. However, Rule 4.2 is necessary because no rule *specifically* grants such right to a Member or obligates the Presiding Officer to recognize a Member's request to speak before the Body.

A request for the Floor must necessarily be made at the appropriate time and in accordance with the *Rules* and local practice. For example, nearly all local governments invoke a system or process for Members to indicate their request to speak, whether that system is by means of a simple show of hands or the use of an electronic queuing system. The use of the local government's established practice or system to request the Floor is a requirement of Rule 4.2. And, when a proper request is made, the Member will be recognized by the Presiding Officer and granted access to the Floor.

When granting the Floor, the Presiding Officer need not be overly formalistic in recognizing a Member. Any recognition that would make it clear that the Member is entitled to speak is sufficient. For example, the Presiding Officer might respond to a Member raising their hand to speak with a simple expression such as "Member A?" or "Member A, did you have a question or comment?" Some Presiding Officers may seek to use a more formal style when recognizing a Member, such as "Member A, you have the Floor." However the Floor is granted, the Presiding Officer should protect the Member's right to the Floor by ensuring an uninterrupted opportunity to speak and calling unauthorized interruptions as out of order. See Rule 4.1.

Rule 4.3
A Member's right to the Floor is limited to five minutes.

Commentary

From the perspective of efficiency and fairness, it is detrimental to the Body for a Member to dominate the available meeting time with lengthy discussion or debate. Based on common local government experience, however, most Members do not often speak for more than five minutes at any one time. But experience also proves that a Member may at times dominate discussion or debate and speak for longer than five minutes. Further, experience proves that Members speaking longer than five minutes at a time are often disorganized or repetitious in conveying the information they seek to present.

Rule 4.3 recognizes that five minutes is typically a sufficient amount of time for a Member to offer viewpoints, opinions, or advocacy during the discussion or debate on a matter or motion.

Nevertheless, a Member may request that the Presiding Officer grant the Member additional time. A Member who knows that their presentation may press the time limit afforded by Rule 4.3 should contact the Presiding Officer in advance of the meeting. Such a request should usually be granted, although setting some reasonable time limitation when granting such a request is appropriate.

A request for more time made during a meeting should customarily be granted by the Presiding Officer unless the Presiding Officer decides that other Members are waiting to be recognized to obtain the Floor or that meeting efficiency necessitates that the requested extension be denied. When the Presiding Officer denies a Member an extension of time to speak, no other Member shall be granted an extension of time for the same agenda item. Moreover, if one Member is granted additional time to speak, other Members making the same request should be treated equally. Speaking more than the allocated time is always out of order.

The Presiding Officer holds the discretion to modify Rule 4.3, with such a modification applying to all Members. A modification may be accomplished through a simple exercise of discretion pursuant to Rule 3.4 or more formally by an announcement of the suspension of the five-minute limitation in accordance with Rule 8.1. A modification may be appropriate given the importance or complexity of the agenda item, the anticipated amount of time available for the agenda, the anticipated time to accommodate citizen participation, and the amount of business that must be accomplished during the meeting. The Presiding Officer's exercise of discretion is subject to a Point of Appeal, and a majority of the Body may affirm or reject the Presiding Officer's decision. See Section 13.0.

Rule 4.4

A Member may obtain the Floor only once until all other Members are offered an opportunity to obtain the Floor.

Commentary

Members are best served by a fair and equitable opportunity to address the Body. Absent a rule to aid the Presiding Officer to monitor access to the Floor, one or more Members can dominate the discussion and debate and potentially suppress or exclude other Members' views.

A Member should only speak once in discussion or debate until all other Members requesting the Floor have an opportunity to speak. The Presiding Officer shall endeavor to equally solicit input from all Members prior to allowing Members who previously obtained the Floor the opportunity to again address the Body.

Obtaining the Floor after previously speaking when other Members are awaiting an opportunity to speak is out of order.

5.0   The Motion & Second

Rule 5.1

A motion is required for the Body to take a formal action.

Commentary

It is axiomatic that the Body may only take formal action through a vote. A vote necessarily requires that a Member offer a motion that proposes a specific request, proposition, or question. Absent a motion and a vote, there is no means available to determine that the Body decided to take a specific action.

For the purposes of Rule 5.1, a formal action is an action to approve or reject an ordinance or a resolution or to render a binding and final decision by the Body that necessarily requires the recording of a vote. The Body's legal counsel should advise the Body regarding those decisions that require a formal motion and a vote. Importantly, Rule 3.4 recognizes the limited authority of the Presiding Officer to use discretion and allow the Body to decide certain administrative and ministerial or minor matters without a formal motion or vote.[71]

Notwithstanding any authority to forgo a formal motion, a formal motion and vote will be available for any action by the Body.[72] A Point of Order or a Point of Appeal are the appropriate means to require compliance with Rule 5.1.

The So Moved Motion

A Member may forgo offering a formal motion by the Member's exclamation of "so moved." The So Moved Motion requires a preceding discussion that the Presiding Officer deems sufficient to clearly define a request, proposition, or question that will be subject to a vote. Upon the exclamation "so moved," the Presiding Officer should summarize or clarify the motion. The So Moved Motion requires a second in accordance with Rule 5.3.

The So Moved Motion will oftentimes follow discussion by the Body or by administrative staff requesting that the Body take a specific action. For example, the Body's finance director may make a presentation to the Body and conclude the presentation with a statement that "the Body is asked to approve the 2026 End of Year Financial Report." To hasten the making of the requested approval, a Member may simply say, "So moved." As another example, a Member may ask for the assistance of legal counsel in fashioning the language of a motion. Upon the legal counsel's verbal suggestion of the language for the motion, a Member may wish to adopt the suggested language as a motion by using the expression "so moved."

Although a Member's opportunity to offer a So Moved Motion should customarily require the Floor, in common practice, the motion is offered spontaneously and then quickly seconded. Provided that the motion does not interrupt another Member who was granted the Floor, and absent a Point of Order objecting to the motion without obtaining the Floor, the Presiding Officer can recognize the motion.

In the event that a Member offers an objection to the use of the So Moved Motion, or a Member offers a Point of Order to require a formal motion in accordance with Rule 5.1, the So Moved Motion shall be disallowed by the Presiding Officer, and a formal motion will be required for the Body to take action.

The Rule in Practice

The following dialogue provides an example of Rule 5.1 in practice, the So Moved Motion, and the use of a Point of Order to require a formal vote:

Background:	The City Manager has the Floor and is presenting an update on current administrative issues.
City Manager:	"I attended a meeting this week with the Student Leadership for Village High School. They gave great reasons why an after-prom party at the high school will best protect our students by offering a safe environment that is monitored better than the various private parties the students might otherwise attend. I request that the City Council support this year's after-prom party and donate $500 to Village High School from the Donation Line Item in our General Fund."
Member A:	"So moved."
Member B:	"Second."
Presiding Officer:	"We have a Principal Motion on the Floor to donate $500 to Village High School for this year's after-prom party to be drawn from our Donations Line Item in the General Fund. Unless there is any further debate on this motion, I will call for the vote."
Member D:	"Point of Order."
Presiding Officer:	"Yes, Member D, what is your Point of Order?"

Member D:	"Our rules of order require a formal motion in order to take action."
Presiding Officer:	"Member D, you are correct. I will disallow the use of a So Moved Motion in this instance. Approval of this requested donation will require a formal motion."

[A formal motion is offered and approved by the Body]

Building upon the previous scenario, the following dialogue provides an example of the Presiding Officer's use of discretion pursuant to Rule 3.4 and the use of a Point of Appeal to challenge the Officer's decision:

Background:	Member D offers a Point of Order to oppose the use of a So Moved Motion and to require a formally stated motion in accordance with Rule 5.1.
Presiding Officer:	"Member D, as the Presiding Officer, I find that the motion is sufficient because our rules of order authorize the use of a So Moved Motion if the Presiding Officer determines that the discussion prior to the motion is sufficient to provide a clear and understandable motion. I find that the So Moved Motion in this case is sufficient for this matter. We can proceed to a debate on the motion."
Member D:	"Point of Appeal. I believe that use of our limited funds in our Donation Line Item of the General Fund justifies a more formal motion and strict adherence to Rule 5.1."

Presiding Officer:	"My decision to accept the So Moved Motion is appealed. An appeal is not debatable. I will call for the vote on the question of whether my decision should be upheld. A "yes" vote is a vote to support my decision and allow the So Moved Motion. A "no" vote is a vote to reject my decision and to require a formal motion. A majority of the quorum is required for this appeal."
	[The Body then proceeds to a vote on the Point of Appeal, and a majority of the quorum supports the Presiding Officer's decision. The So Moved Motion is then debated and decided.]

Rule 5.2

A motion shall propose an affirmative proposition in clear and understandable language that is limited to either a "yes" or a "no" vote.

Commentary

Rule 5.2 establishes three requirements for a proper motion: (1) an affirmative proposition that is (2) stated in clear and understandable language and that (3) calls for a "yes" or a "no" vote.

✦ Affirmative Proposition

Motions ask the Body to make a decision. For all motions other than a Principal Motion, the motions are each limited by the motion's required language and purpose to ask that the Body decide to take an *affirmative* or positive action—that is, upon the approval of the motion, the Body will change the existing state of affairs in the course of the meeting.

Unlike the other motions, Principal Motions are not necessarily limited to a request to take affirmative action. Although most Principal Motions will propose that the Body take an affirmative action, a Principal Motion could potentially ask the Body to not take an action. A motion proposing that the Body not take action is unnecessary, if not confusing. The Body need not approve a motion in order to maintain the status quo. As an example, a Principal Motion "to not take a recess," if approved, would not change the status quo and would merely confirm the state of affairs that would exist in the absence of the motion.

Rule 5.2 requires that all motions propose that the Body take an affirmative or positive action, the approval of which will change the status quo. Requiring all motions to seek an affirmative action is entirely consistent with local government's customary approach to governance. Most agenda items either expressly or implicitly ask that the Body consider approving the taking of action. And, notably, a "motion to approve" an action is by far the most common form of motion.

Requiring an affirmative motion promotes efficiency. An affirmative motion enables the Body to reach a decisive or final decision regardless of the vote to approve or reject the motion. See Rules 7.7 and 7.8.

✦ Clear and Understandable Language

On occasion, a Moving Member may propose a confusing motion that other Members do not clearly understand. Confusion is often the product of an overly wordy or a multipart motion.

When motions are imprecise, unclear, or not fully understood by the Body, the Body's decision can mean different things to different

Members. Members may later dispute the motion's intent or scope and the specific action directed by the Body. The administrative staff may find it difficult to carry out the directions of a confusing or unclear motion. A concise, clear, and understandable motion is the goal, if not an absolute necessity.

When a Member is uncertain about the purpose or meaning of a motion, it is appropriate to offer a Point of Information seeking an explanation from the Moving Member. The Body benefits from clarity in the motion. Inquiries into the purpose or meaning of the motion can oftentimes result in the withdrawal of the motion or a more understandable restatement of the motion.

✦ "Yes" or "No" Vote

A motion will be ineffective to direct action unless the motion asks for a simple and unconditional "yes" or "no" vote.[73] A motion that requires the Members to explain a position or an opinion will not likely lead to a definitive decision by the Body. Consider, for example, a motion that states, "I move to have the Trustees identify how much they would support funding Trustee education and training for each of the next four years." It is highly likely that the Trustees will offer a variety of different opinions in response to the motion. This motion does not allow the Members to vote "yes" or "no" and is therefore out of order.

Special Note: Lack of an Offer of a Motion to Approve

On rare occasions, the Members of the Body may be unwilling to offer a Principal Motion "to approve" a proposed action. This unwillingness may be the result of strong or unanimous opposition to the approval of the requested action. Although a Principal Motion "to deny" the proposed action remains a possibility, a motion to approve the action can be more efficient. A motion to approve that fails to receive the necessary vote will result in a definitive or decisive decision to reject the motion's proposition in accordance with Rule 7.8.

The *Rules of Order* provides an assurance that a motion to approve can serve the Body notwithstanding a Moving Member's opposition to the motion. Rule 7.4 recognizes that the offer of a motion does not require the Moving Member to advocate in favor of the motion or to vote to approve the motion. Additionally, Rule 5.6 affords a Moving Member the first right to speak to the motion. This opportunity allows the Moving Member to state at the outset of the motion's consideration that the Member is offering the motion to allow the Body to debate and that the Moving Member will likely be voting against the motion. Simply stated, the offer of a motion to approve will not imply that the motion should be, or will be, approved by the Body. The motion is, however, the most efficient approach to deciding general propositions for action presented to the Body.

Rule 5.3
A motion requires a second.

Commentary

A motion must receive a second before any debate may commence. The reason for this rule is efficiency. A second is an expression of support by a Member that the motion should be entertained by the Body. It is inefficient for the Body to devote time or effort debating a proposed motion that no Member other than the Moving Member supports for consideration and debate.

But, very importantly, the offer of a second is not an expression that the Member offering the second approves or supports the motion's proposition. The Member offering a second only desires to open debate on the motion. A Member's offer of a second does not preclude the Member from later opposing or voting against the seconded motion. See Rule 7.4.

As a limited expression of support for debate, the second does not require that the Member obtain the Floor, and, moreover, the offer of a second does not grant the Floor to the Member. The expression "second," "I second," or a similar affirmative declaration is appropriate, and any other expression or attempt to comment on the motion is out of order.

The Presiding Officer should await the offer of a second before acknowledging the motion pursuant to Rule 5.4. It is also helpful for the Presiding Officer to ask for a second on a motion, which can highlight for the Members the need for a second before proceeding. The lack of a second after allowing a reasonable time for the second will result in the motion's failure. In this case, the Presiding Officer should declare that "the motion dies for lack of a second," the declaration of which will remove the motion from any further consideration. A new motion would then be in order, or, if a new motion is not offered, the Presiding Officer may move to the next agenda item.

Special Note: Quasi-Judicial Matters – Lack of a Second

For a quasi-judicial matter, the applicant is legally entitled to a final decision from the Body. The lack of a second, and the resulting failure of the motion, does not provide a definitive or final decision. The failure of the second simply means that a particular motion will not be placed on the Floor. Upon the failure of the motion to receive a second, the Presiding Officer should request a new motion that will lead to the Body satisfying the requirement for a final decision on the quasi-judicial matter.

Rule 5.4

To be placed on the Floor for the Body's consideration, the Presiding Officer must acknowledge that the motion was properly stated and seconded in accordance with Rules 5.2 and 5.3.

Commentary

Rule 5.4 advances meeting efficiency. The Rule permits the Presiding Officer an opportunity to determine that a motion satisfies the requirements of Rule 5.2 (properly stated) and Rule 5.3 (properly seconded). The Presiding Officer should promptly make the determination and, when justified, acknowledge the motion. Upon acknowledgement, the motion will be on the Floor for the Body's consideration and debate.

The Presiding Officer's acknowledgment of a motion may be formal ("We have a motion properly stated and seconded which proposes approval of Ordinance No. 23, and the motion is now on the Floor") or informal ("Does anyone wish to speak to the motion?"). To enhance the Body's understanding of the motion, it is helpful if the Presiding Officer restates or summarizes the motion upon its acknowledgement.

Rule 5.4 allows the Presiding Officer and the Members an opportunity to address any deficiencies in the form of the motion prior to the motion being placed on the Floor. For example, when the motion's language is not clear and understandable, the motion, even if seconded, is not yet on the Floor. The Presiding Officer and the Members of the Body can bring to the Moving Party's attention the motion's lack of clarity. The Moving Member is then provided an opportunity to change or even withdraw the motion. See Rule 5.5. When the motion is changed appropriately, the motion can be seconded, and the Presiding Officer can acknowledge the motion.

If the Presiding Officer withholds acknowledgement of a properly stated and seconded motion, a Point of Order or Point of Appeal is available to challenge the Presiding Officer's lack of action.

Rule 5.5

A motion, once acknowledged by the Presiding Officer and placed on the Floor, is owned by the Body.

Commentary

A Moving Member may attempt during debate to exercise control over a motion by unilaterally modifying the motion's language or by proclaiming the motion as withdrawn from consideration. Some local governments condone this practice under an assumption that the Moving Member holds some form of right, ownership, or control over the motion until it receives a final vote. This practice is ill-advised.

Rule 5.5 recognizes a specific point in time when ownership and control over a motion will rest with the Body. A motion is not on the Floor and capable of any consideration and debate until the Presiding Officer acknowledges the motion in accordance with Rule 5.4. Until this acknowledgement, the Moving Member may change or withdraw the motion. A change or withdrawal may typically be made in response to inquiries about the motion from the Presiding Officer or the Members. But, upon the Presiding Officer's acknowledgement, the Body will own and control the motion, and the Moving Member cannot change or withdraw the motion.

To allow the Moving Member to unilaterally change or withdraw a motion on the Floor can be problematic. Once on the Floor, the Body will devote time debating the motion. Members will take positions on the motion and may demand that the Body reach a final decision to approve or reject the motion. Moreover, the Members may propose one or more amendments to the motion to best express the Members' positions. If a Moving Member retains control over a motion, the Moving Member may unilaterally control the Body's ability to render a decision by changing or withdrawing the motion. Rule 5.5 helps prevent a Moving Member from unilaterally undermining the Body's decision-making process.

Rule 5.6

The Presiding Officer shall offer the Moving Member the first opportunity to speak to a debatable motion.

Commentary

Once on the Floor, a debatable[74] motion can proceed to debate. As the principal proponent of the motion, the Moving Member is afforded the first opportunity to address the purpose and need for the motion. The explanation may help focus the Body's debate and may highlight a need for amendment to ensure that the motion aligns with the Moving Member's intent or serves the Body's goals.

Rule 5.6 neither requires the Moving Member to accept the Presiding Officer's invitation to address the motion nor precludes the Moving Member from later addressing the motion during debate as permitted by Rule 4.2.

6.0 The Friendly Requests

Rule 6.1

A Friendly Amendment is authorized only for a debatable motion, and the amendment of the motion will be effective unless a Member objects.

Commentary

The need to amend a motion is common. Some amendments may be complex—for example, an amendment of a motion to add conditions to the approval of a proposed land use. For these more complex amendments, the proper amendment procedure is a Motion to Amend. See Section 17.0, Motion to Amend.

However, some amendments may be as simple as asking for a change of a word, a number, or a date. For example, consider a Principal Motion to approve the purchase of seven new laptop computers for the governing body's use. A Member may offer a Motion to Amend the Principal Motion to change the number of laptops from seven to eight to supply the Body with a backup unit. This simple amendment is clear and understandable and would not require much, if any, debate. It is also an amendment that may be readily acceptable to all the Members of the Body. Therefore, a simplified and informal procedure to amend a motion can advance meeting efficiency.[75] The Friendly Amendment fulfills this role.

A Friendly Amendment is only available to amend a debatable[76] motion. A Friendly Amendment is out of order when offered to amend a motion that is not debatable. A Friendly Amendment enables the Presiding Officer to exercise discretion and to forgo a formal Motion to Amend, a debate, and a vote. Because Rule 5.1 requires a motion for the Body to take action, the Friendly Amendment is effectively a special exception to Rule 5.1.

The Friendly Amendment is initiated by a request that includes the specific amendment proposed. In the preceding example concerning laptop computers, the request for a Friendly Amendment may state, "I request a Friendly Amendment to change the number of laptops from seven to eight."

Any Member, including the Presiding Officer, may request a Friendly Amendment. The request requires that the Member have the Floor.

Importantly, it is the Presiding Officer, not the Moving Member who offered the original motion, who may approve a request for a Friendly Amendment. This approach is entirely appropriate given that the Body owns the motion on the Floor, not the Moving Member. See Rule 5.5. Moreover, the Presiding Officer is already empowered to assume the Floor and to exercise discretion to advance meeting efficiency.

Upon the announcement of the request, the Presiding Officer should await an objection and, hearing none, declare that the motion on the Floor is amended as stated in the request for the Friendly Amendment. It is the absence of an objection from any Member of the Body that effectively renders the amendment "friendly."

When the Friendly Amendment is not unanimously supported by the Members, a simple exclamation of "objection" by a Member will make the Friendly Amendment unavailable to the Body.[77] An objection will effectively require the Body to either abandon the requested amendment or resort to a formal Motion to Amend, debate, and a vote if the amendment is to move forward. See Section 17.0, Motion to Amend.

The Rule in Practice

The following dialogue provides an example of Rule 6.1 in practice:

Background:	The Town Manager presents Ordinance 19 to the Town Board. Ordinance 19 will amend the Town Code and require all dogs to be kept on a minimum ten-foot leash when outside of a building or outside of a fenced yard.
Member A:	[Who was granted the Floor by the Presiding Officer] "I move to approve Ordinance 19 as presented."
Member B:	"Second."
Presiding Officer:	"We have a Principal Motion on the Floor to approve Ordinance 19 as presented. This motion is debatable. Member A, you have the right to speak first on the motion. Would you like to speak to your motion?"
Member A:	"No, thank you."
Member C:	[Who was granted the Floor by the Presiding Officer] "I believe that, in the study session on this issue, we supported a maximum eight-foot leash because it was the standard used by other communities and is a safe length for control of a dog. I request that the Presiding Officer accept a Friendly Amendment to the motion to change the phrase in Ordinance 19 that currently states 'a maximum of ten feet' to instead state 'a maximum of eight feet.'"

Presiding Officer: "Thank you, Member C. I agree with your suggested amendment and accept the Friendly Amendment to change the maximum length of the leash from ten feet to eight feet.

"Is there any objection to this friendly amendment?

"Hearing no objection, the motion to approve Ordinance 19, as amended by the Friendly Amendment, now states the leash must be 'a maximum of eight feet' and is now on the Floor for debate."

[The Body then continues in debate on the Principal Motion as amended by the Friendly Amendment. Note that a formal Motion to Amend would be available if the Presiding Officer rejected the request for a Friendly Amendment or an objection to the Friendly Amendment was raised by a Member.]

Rule 6.2

A Friendly Withdrawal is authorized only for a debatable motion, and the withdrawal of the motion will be effective unless a Member objects.

Commentary

A majority of the Members may find a proposed motion on the Floor to be unacceptable. For such a motion, the common method to effectively withdraw the motion from the Floor is by a vote on the motion as presented and the motion's failure to receive the necessary number of votes for approval.

On occasion, however, the Body may recognize during debate that a debatable motion will not enable the Body to reach a meaningful conclusion and that an entirely different motion—or no motion at all—should be offered. For example, the debate on a Principal Motion proposing to fund a city council retreat may demonstrate that only the Moving Member desires to attend a retreat. In the face of this apparent strong opposition to the retreat, continuing debate on the motion is unwarranted, pointless, or inefficient. In this instance, Rule 6.2 authorizes a "Friendly Withdrawal" to promote meeting efficiency.

The Friendly Withdrawal is only available for a debatable[78] motion. The reason for this limitation is that a nondebatable motion will not present an opportunity for Members to access the Floor and express opinions on the motion. A nondebatable motion will immediately proceed to a vote without debate. When sufficient opposition to the nondebatable motion exists, the motion will be promptly and efficiently rejected by a vote.

A Friendly Withdrawal is initiated by a Member's request or by the Presiding Officer. Upon the announcement of the request to consider a Friendly Withdrawal, the Presiding Officer should await an objection from a Member and, hearing none, declare the motion on the Floor withdrawn. It is the absence of an objection from a Member of the Body that effectively renders the withdrawal "friendly."[79]

Importantly, it is the Presiding Officer and not the Moving Member who may approve a request to withdraw a motion by a Friendly Withdrawal. This approach is entirely appropriate given that a motion on the Floor is owned by the Body, not the Moving Member. See Rule 5.5. Moreover, the Presiding Officer is authorized to exercise discretion to advance meeting efficiency. See Rule 3.4.

Upon a Member's timely objection to a proposed Friendly Withdrawal, the Friendly Withdrawal is unavailable, and the pending motion must proceed to a formal decision by the Body.

The Rule in Practice

The following dialogue provides an example of Rule 6.2 in practice:

Background: Member A offered a Principal Motion to approve an application for a special-use permit for an animal hospital. The motion included several conditions regarding the operation of the hospital. The motion received a second and was acknowledged by the Presiding Officer as properly on the Floor. After some debate on the motion, the Body recognized that the motion would require significant and time-consuming amendment to bring the motion into a form that the Body could reasonably entertain. Another Member suggested "scrapping" the pending Principal Motion and starting over with a different motion for approval. A majority of the Members expressed strong support for the suggestion to "scrap" the motion.

Member A: [Who was granted the Floor] "After hearing the comments during debate that this motion needs a lot of work if we are going to reach a final decision, I request that the Presiding Officer accept a Friendly Withdrawal of the motion."

Presiding Officer: "Member A has asked for a Friendly Withdrawal of the motion. I agree that withdrawing this motion is necessary so we can take a different approach with a new motion. Unless there is an objection, I will withdraw the motion.

"Hearing no objection, the motion to approve the conditional-use application is withdrawn. Do we have any other motion or request?"

Using the same scenario for the Principal Motion to approve the special-use permit for the animal hospital, the following dialogue illustrates the use of an objection to defeat a proposal for a Friendly Withdrawal:

Member A:	[Who was granted the Floor] "After hearing the comments during debate that this motion needs a lot of work to reach a final decision, I request that the Presiding Officer accept a Friendly Withdrawal of the motion."
Presiding Officer:	"Member A has asked for a Friendly Withdrawal of the motion. I agree with the request. Unless there is an objection, I will withdraw the motion."
Member C:	"Objection."
Presiding Officer:	"Member C objects to the use of the Friendly Withdrawal in this instance. A Friendly Withdrawal is not available for this motion.
	[The Body then proceeds to a formal vote on the Principal Motion, which is rejected, and the Body then entertains a new motion.]

7.0. The Vote

Rule 7.1

The Presiding Officer's call for the vote closes the Floor.

Commentary

The debate of a proposed motion may at times seem never-ending, with Members repeatedly seeking the Floor and often repeating the same comments in support or opposition to the motion. At other times, the debate is succinct, or Members know their vote without debate. Eventually, the Presiding Officer must call for the vote to enable the Body to render a decision.

Absent a rule that will close the Floor, Members may request the Floor and engage the Body in debate even during the voting process. The call for the vote is a declaration that the Floor is no longer open to prevent the interruption of the process of voting. No Member is authorized to seek the Floor or to speak to the Body following the call for the vote.

However, Rule 7.1 does not preclude a Point of Order, Point of Information, or Point of Appeal, which remain available to Members as privileged actions that can allow the Body to address urgent matters concerning meeting process.

The Presiding Officer's decision to call for the vote is a discretionary decision subject to a Point of Appeal. A successful appeal will cause the Floor to remain open until the Presiding Officer again calls for the vote or the Body approves a Motion to Close Debate. See Section 18.0.

Rule 7.2

Proxy or absentee voting is not permitted.

Commentary

Rule 7.2 effectively limits voting to only Members in attendance.[80] Rule 7.2 also directly advances the public policy established by the Colorado Open Meetings Law that the business conducted by elected and appointed officials occurs in meetings that are open to the public. Proxy and absentee voting undermine the openness and transparency of government.

Voting by proxy allows a Member to vote on behalf of another Member.[81] Proxy voting undermines or defeats equality among Members by granting the Member holding a proxy greater voting power than other Members. The proxy grants a Member two or more votes. Moreover, in circumstances where the Member granting the proxy limits or conditions the voting authority of the proxy holder, the Body has no means to ensure that the proxy vote is cast correctly—that is, unless the Body undertakes a review of any written proxy form or confirms any limits or conditions with the Member granting the proxy. Reviewing or confirming the proxy will obviously delay the meeting and reduce efficiency. Proxies that are unclear as to the proxy holder's scope of authority to vote will place the Presiding Officer or the Body in the position of judging the intent or validity of the proxy prior to the casting of the vote. If the goals of a meeting are fairness to the Members and efficiency, proxy voting is antithetical to such goals.

Absentee voting allows a Member to submit a vote on a matter in advance of the meeting. The *Rules of Order* prohibits absentee voting because the vote lacks the confidence of being a fully informed and well-reasoned decision. Most obviously, the absent Member may prepare and submit their vote for a motion, proposition, or question that is not likely known to the absent Member. An absentee Member will also not be aware of any information, testimony, evidence, discussion, and debate offered during the meeting and prior to the vote. In a quasi-judicial matter, an absentee vote can show that the absent Member pre-judged the matter or held a bias or prejudice based on information the absent Member obtained outside of the quasi-judicial hearing. Such prejudgment, bias, or prejudice can undermine the fairness owed to the applicant and the meeting participants required by procedural due process.[82]

Rule 7.3

A Member may not explain their vote after the call for the vote.

Commentary

Several rules effectively limit a Member's ability to explain their vote after the Presiding Officer's call for the vote. Rule 4.1 requires the Floor to address the Body, Rule 7.1 closes the Floor upon the call for the vote, and Rule 7.5 limits a Member to the expression of a "yes" or "no" vote on a motion. Nevertheless, Members may try to use the voting opportunity to explain the reasoning or basis for their vote. This practice is both inefficient and ill-advised.

Rule 7.3 advances the efficiency of both the process of debate and the process of voting. During debate, Members enjoy a full opportunity to explain why they support or oppose a motion. Members have a right to the Floor, may speak for five minutes, and may obtain the Floor multiple times during debate. See Rules 4.2, 4.3, and 4.4. If a Member did not exercise the full and available opportunity to explain their position and their vote during debate, it is reasonable to deny the Member an opportunity to explain a vote when a vote is cast.

Rule 7.3 enhances the quality of the decision-making process by discouraging a Member from remaining silent during debate. A silent Member deprives the Body of the Member's reasoning that supports the Member's vote. When a silent Member explains a vote after the close of debate, the other Members cannot obtain the Floor to support or rebut the previously silent Member's reasoning. If a Member has already cast a vote and then finds the silent Member's explanation persuasive, the Member may wish to change the earlier vote, which can lead to meeting dysfunction.

Many Bodies use a roll-call system to cast votes, and, for these Bodies, attempts to use the voting opportunity to explain a vote are more commonplace. For Bodies using voting machines or other mechanical methods that require each Member to cast a vote simultaneously, these voting methods can help prevent the late explanation of a vote. However, as Members cast their vote by pressing a button or flipping a switch, it is possible that the Member will use that time to announce the reasons why they are casting their vote.

Regardless of the local government's system for voting, Rule 7.3 clarifies that any attempt to explain a vote at the time of the casting of the vote is out of order.

Rule 7.4

Neither the Moving Member nor the Member offering a second on a motion must advocate or vote in favor of the motion.

Commentary

Some bodies require a Member offering a motion and the Member seconding a motion to advocate in favor of the motion. A few bodies require these Members to ultimately vote in favor of the motion. These practices may stem from a belief that the Members will both support and vote to approve the motion because these Members initially offered or supported the motion. The practice may also be based on an adopted rule of order that obligates the Moving Member and the Member offering a second to support the proposed motion.[83]

Rule 7.4 clarifies that the mere offering of a motion or the offering of a second does not limit Members to a particular position or vote. Rule 7.4 makes common sense. After offering a motion or offering a second, a Member may be persuaded during the debate that the motion will not achieve the Member's intended goal. In addition, amendments to the motion may result in a Member deciding to oppose the motion. And, at times, a Member may initially offer a motion for the purpose of allowing debate and with the intent that the Body will see the wisdom of rejecting the motion.[84]

Rule 7.4 recognizes that the offering of a motion, and the offering of the second, only means that the Moving Member and the Member offering the second intend that the Body debate the motion's proposition.

Rule 7.5

Each Member eligible to vote on a motion shall vote either "yes" or "no."

Commentary

Because Rule 5.2 requires the form of a motion to require a "yes" or a "no" vote,[85] Members are limited when voting to declare unconditional support or opposition to the motion. To be successful, a motion must receive the required number of "yes" votes to approve the motion. See Rule 7.6.

On occasion, a Member eligible to vote as part of the quorum of the Body may seek to "abstain" at the time of the vote. An abstention is an act to avoid voting or to not vote.[86] The desire to abstain may be due to a variety of reasons, which may include the Member feeling unprepared to vote due to a lack of information or the Member's desire to simply not be placed "on the record" in support or opposition of a proposition. It is important to recognize that abstaining from a vote is different than not voting due to a conflict of interest. A conflict of interest requires the conflicted Member's exclusion from the quorum, exclusion from participation in the matter, and exclusion from the vote. See Rule 1.4. In contrast, abstaining refers to the Member's decision to not cast a vote when the Member has no legal reason that would prevent the Member's participation in the matter or prevent the casting of a vote.

Rule 7.5 does not recognize a right to abstain from a vote.[87] Whether a Member is elected or appointed to serve the Body, the *Rules* assumes that the Member's acceptance of the position is a commitment to perform the duties of the position unless such performance is prevented by law.[88] The ultimate exercise of the Member's duty is the casting of a vote on a motion to allow the Body to make a decision. An abstention, regardless of its reason, is a disregard of the duty voluntarily accepted by the elected or appointed Member to represent the public.

In the event that a Member eligible to vote abstains or otherwise refuses to cast a "yes" or "no" vote in accordance with Rule 7.5, the vote is out of order. The Presiding Officer may ask the abstaining or nonvoting Member to vote in accordance with Rule 7.5 by declaring a "yes" or a "no" vote. Should the Member refuse to vote in accordance with Rule 7.5, the Body may consider recording the failure to vote in the minutes as, for example, "Member Smith refused to vote."[89] The failure to vote will not count as either a "yes" or a "no" vote.

Some local government bodies follow a rule or bylaw provision that requires the recording of an abstention or other refusal to vote as either a "yes" or a "no" vote. The Body should consult its legal counsel in any decision to impute a vote to a nonvoting Member. This issue has a long, although not recent or extensive, history of legal precedent.[90]

Special Note: Approval of the Minutes

A Member may want to abstain from a vote on a motion to approve the minutes from a prior meeting solely because the Member was absent from the meeting. The Member may feel that, due to their absence, they cannot personally attest to the accuracy of the minutes.

The rule requiring a previously absent Member to vote "yes" or "no" on the approval of the minutes is not necessarily inconsistent. A previously absent Member may vote "yes" to approve the minutes because the Member has no reason or justification to object to the content of the minutes.

Additionally, an absent Member may rely upon a common presumption that the clerk or other administrative staff person charged with the taking of the minutes accurately recorded the meeting minutes. It is exceedingly rare that an error in the minutes creates conflict. An inaccuracy in the minutes, when noted by a Member, is usually corrected prior to the motion and the Body's vote to approve. A previously absent Member may readily observe that the absence of any objection by other Members to the minutes, or the correction of the minutes to resolve any inaccuracy, will justify a "yes" vote for approval.

Rule 7.6

The approval of a motion requires a vote of a majority of a quorum unless a greater number of votes is required by the *Rules of Order* or by law.

Commentary

The common rule for a motion is that the majority of a quorum[91] in attendance is necessary to decide the motion's outcome. This is a default rule because some motions require a different and higher voting standard.[92] The common rule gives exception to three motions:

+ Motion to Close Debate, which requires a two-thirds (2/3) vote of a quorum. See Section 18.0.

+ Motion to Reconsider, which requires a two-thirds (2/3) vote of a quorum. See Section 19.0.

+ Motion for Executive Session, which requires a two-thirds (2/3) vote of a quorum.[93] See Section 22.0.

These three motions can effectively deprive Members of important rights associated with the decision-making process or deprive the public of the right to observe the decision-making process. As a result, a higher or supermajority voting requirement is justified.

Additionally, special statutory voting requirements impose added exceptions to the common rule. The Body should consult the Body's attorney to identify the special voting requirements of state law and whether the requirements are applicable to the Body.

By way of some examples, potential statutory modifications of the common rule for a majority vote of a quorum include:

+ Municipal ordinances, resolutions, and orders for the appropriation of money requires approval by a majority of the governing body and not a majority of a quorum.[94]

+ For municipalities having adopted the necessary ordinance to require the mayor's signature on any ordinance adopted and all resolutions authorizing the expenditure of money or entering into a contract, a mayoral disapproval and refusal to sign the ordinance or resolution may be overridden by a two-thirds (2/3) affirmative vote of the Members of the governing body.[95]

+ Adoption of an emergency ordinance requires a vote of three-fourths (3/4) of the Members of the governing body of the municipality.[96]

+ Colorado state law requires a two-thirds (2/3) vote of all the Members of the governing body of a municipality to approve a change in zoning or zoning regulations in the event of a properly filed protest.[97]

+ The Colorado Open Meetings Law requires a two-thirds (2/3) vote of a quorum to hold an Executive Session.[98] This same voting requirement is set forth in Section 22.0 of these *Rules*.

Lastly, home-rule charters and local ordinances may also impose special voting requirements on the Body. For example, in one home-rule municipality, a vote to authorize the exercise of the power of eminent domain to take possession of private property requires a vote of two-thirds (2/3) of all Members of the city council in office at the time of the vote.[99]

Rule 7.7

The approval of a motion by the required vote shall decisively approve the motion's proposition or question.

Commentary

Rule 7.7 works in cooperation with Rule 7.6, which sets the number of votes required for approval of a motion. Rule 7.7 provides that the Body's approval of a motion by a vote of the required majority will decisively approve the motion's proposition or question.

Rule 7.8

The failure of a motion to receive the required vote for approval shall decisively disapprove the motion's proposition.

Commentary

Rule 7.8 recognizes the obvious result of a vote that fails to gain the majority vote for approval, the failure of which also includes a tie vote. Because the motion must state an affirmative proposition as required by Rule 5.2, the failure of the vote on the motion will decisively disapprove the motion's proposition to take action. In effect, the question presented is "Shall the Body approve the motion's proposition?" and the resulting answer by the failure of the Body to gain the required majority's vote is a decisive "no."

Special Note: Motion to Deny

A special mention is warranted for a "Motion to Deny." This motion is often proposed during the consideration of a quasi-judicial matter to approve an application. For example, the motion might state, "I move to deny the application requesting a rezoning of Lot 9 to the R-1 Zone District."

In accordance with Rule 7.7, the Body's vote to approve the Motion to Deny the rezoning application will result in a decisive decision to deny the requested rezoning. That is, the Body was asked by the motion, "Shall we deny the application?" and the answer of the Body is "Yes, we will deny the application." The requested rezoning is denied or rejected and the decision is final.

But what happens when the Body *does not* gain the votes necessary to approve a Motion to Deny? The Body's failure to approve a Motion to Deny only rejects the motion's request. In the example of the rezoning of Lot 9, the failure to approve the Motion to Deny only rejects the request to deny the rezoning of Lot 9.

Critically important is that—by not gaining the votes needed to deny the motion—the Body is *not approving* the motion. The Motion to Deny only asked the Body, "Shall we deny the application?" and the Body's answer is "No, we will not deny the application." The Body was not asked to approve the application. So, the application which requested the

Body's approval of the rezoning remains before the Body for a decision. Note that, if the failure of a Motion to Deny could result in an approval, then a tie vote on the Motion to Deny would approve an application. It would be unacceptable for less than a majority of the Body to render a decisive or final decision.

To reach a definitive decision following the failure of a Motion to Deny requires that the Body be asked to approve the rezoning. Upon the presentation of a motion to approve the rezoning application, and pursuant to Rule 7.7, the vote on the Motion to Approve will result in a definitive decision on the requested rezoning whether the motion receives the required vote or not.

Rule 7.9

A Member shall not change their vote after the announcement of the final vote except in exceptional circumstances with the approval of the Presiding Officer.

Commentary

The purpose of Rule 7.9 is to ensure the finality of a vote by the Body. If one or more votes can be changed after the final vote is announced, the decision cannot be deemed final. The only means to ensure finality is through a rule prohibiting a change in vote.

The appropriate method to reconsider a vote and to enter a new vote following final announcement would be a successful Motion to Reconsider. See Section 19.0. The successful Motion to Reconsider would reopen the prior matter, rescind the prior final decision, and enable the Members to propose the same or a different motion and effectively provide an opportunity to change a vote.

Rule 7.9 requires an exception to address circumstances related to deficiencies in the voting method or a reasonable accommodation for a Member's disability. It is foreseeable that a Member may cast a vote only to learn after the vote announcement that their vote was not properly recorded. For example, a poor audio system associated with a video conference or remote meeting may at times fail to allow a Member to clearly record a vote due to multiple speakers voting simultaneously. Additionally, an error in voting may be made by a person with a visual or hearing impairment due to pressing the wrong voting button or indicating a vote at the wrong moment. The Presiding Officer is authorized to recognize the need to allow for changes in votes in such exceptional circumstances.

Special Note: Changing a Vote During the Voting Process

Related to Rule 7.9 is a Member's attempt to change a vote during the voting process but *before* the announcement of the final vote. Rule 7.9 does not prohibit a change of a vote prior to the announcement.

Nevertheless, allowing a Member to change a vote after the vote is cast is problematic. The practice conveys an appearance that the Member changed the vote not based on a reconsideration of the information, evidence, or advocacy presented during the meeting but because the Member is responding to the vote of another Member. In addition, the practice is disfavored because the Member seeking to change a vote may do so to manipulate the outcome in the event of a close vote. However, a Member may seek to change a vote prior to the final announcement of the vote simply because the Member misunderstood the motion or cast an incorrect vote due to a recognized disability. Rule 7.9 allows the Presiding Officer to accommodate a justifiable need to change a vote.

To address the issue of changing votes during the voting process and to introduce equality in the voting process, some local governments use voting equipment or tools that require Members to cast their votes simultaneously. All votes cast are displayed at the same time immediately prior to the announcement of the final vote. This method reduces or eliminates the potential for the changing of a vote based upon another Member's vote or to manipulate the outcome in a close vote.

8.0   Rule Suspension and Rule Deviation

Rule 8.1
The Presiding Officer may suspend certain rules.

Commentary

Rule 8.1, together with the Presiding Officer's general authority to exercise discretion (Rule 3.4), allows the Presiding Officer to suspend certain rules of order. The purpose of this authority is to advance meeting efficiency and to address special circumstances arising during a meeting or for an agenda item where the Body does not object to the suspension of the rule by an appeal of the Presiding Officer's decision.

The Presiding Officer may suspend only the following rules:

✦ Rule 1.2

The meeting agenda will be followed unless properly amended or modified.

The Presiding Officer may recognize that flexibility is needed in following the agenda to accommodate the planned late arrival of a Member; the availability of necessary staff, applicants, or speakers; or for other reasons related to efficiency. Rule 8.1 authorizes the Presiding Officer to suspend the requirement that the agenda be followed in the order presented.

✦ Rule 3.1

The Presiding Officer shall be the exclusive director and facilitator of all meeting conduct.

Suspension of Rule 3.1 may be appropriate when the Presiding Officer seeks a greater and active role in the discussion or debate on a matter that may be inconsistent with the Officer's general obligation to facilitate the meeting in a fair and neutral manner. See Rule 3.5. Rule 8.1 allows the Presiding Officer to "pass the gavel" to another Member in accordance with the Body's rules of procedure.

✦ Rule 4.1

The Floor is required to address the Body.

On occasion, forgoing the need to obtain the Floor can enable the Body to engage in a more freeform discussion on a topic.

✦ Rule 4.3

A Member's right to the Floor is limited to five minutes.

Some topics before the Body will generate significant discussion and debate, which may be hampered by Rule 4.3 and the time restriction for a Member's access to the Floor. Suspension of Rule 4.3 can alleviate the Members' concerns for meeting time limitations when offering comment or advocacy.

✦ Rule 4.4

A Member may obtain the Floor only once until other Members are afforded an opportunity.

Invariably, a topic before the Body for discussion or debate will be of far greater concern, if not passion, for one or a few Members. Those concerned or passionate Members oftentimes are better prepared to present relevant information to the Body that brings about a more focused or robust discussion. Where the Presiding Officer recognizes this concern or passion, a suspension of Rule 4.4 can grant to all Members the opportunity to more fully express their concerns, and the Body may generally benefit from the suspension.

✦ Rule 7.3

A Member's attempt to explain their vote after the call for the vote is not permitted.

Some debatable motions may not necessitate extensive debate. As an alternative, simple statements at the time of the cast of the vote will be an efficient means of memorializing the Members' opinions. Rule 8.1 allows the Presiding Officer to open the call for the vote to Members to explain their vote at the time of voting. The Presiding

Officer may wish to provide direction that the suspension is offered to forgo extensive debate for the purpose of efficiency and that the Members are to limit their explanations to summary statements.

✦ Rule 14.3
Only one Motion to Amend may be on the Floor at any one time.

The Presiding Officer may recognize circumstances where a Principal Motion will require a greater degree of modification by the Members to bring about a more effective, comprehensive, or acceptable decision by the Body. For example, some quasi-judicial matters will generate debate on a Principal Motion that integrates the Members' detailed evaluation of the presentations and evidence, and the evaluation may culminate in a variety of needed refinements to the motion. Suspending Rule 14.3 may provide flexibility to fashion a more refined motion, although the Presiding Officer should remain aware that a balance is needed between allowing debate on multiple amendments with the confusion that these proposed amendments may present for the Body. Suspension of Rule 14.3 to permit a limited number of amendments, e.g., only two on the Floor at one time, may be a reasonable approach.

The Presiding Officer's discretion in suspending a rule is subject to a Point of Appeal. The Point of Appeal effectively places the authority to suspend a rule in the hands of the Body, and, if a majority of the Body deems the exercise of authority appropriate or inappropriate, the Body's decision will govern the Presiding Officer's ability to suspend a rule.

Very importantly, the Presiding Officer shall not be authorized to suspend or alter any other rule and, in particular, the following:

+ The availability of a point or a motion to the Body.

+ The requirements or limitations established for a point or motion (e.g., whether the point does not require the Floor, a motion is or is not debatable or amendable, etc.).

+ The vote required for any motion (majority, supermajority). Rule 7.5.

+ The prohibition against proxy or absentee voting. Rule 7.2.

Rule 8.2
The Body may suspend certain rules.

Commentary

The Body may, by use of a Principal Motion with a majority vote of the quorum, suspend a rule of order subject to the same restrictions imposed by Rule 8.1 on the Presiding Officer's authority to suspend.

Rule 8.3
An inadvertent and non-substantive deviation from a rule by the Presiding Officer or the Body without objection from a Member is authorized and intended.

Commentary

From time to time, the Body's meeting conduct will inadvertently deviate from the requirements of a rule. For example, one or more

Members may speak during an agenda item for more than five minutes contrary to Rule 4.3, or the Presiding Officer may allow a Member the Floor to speak twice prior to opening the Floor to other Members contrary to Rule 4.4. However, the Members and the Presiding Officer may elect to not call the deviation to the attention of the Body to address or correct the deviation.

In the event that the Body deviates from the requirements of the *Rules of Order* without an objection from the Presiding Officer or a Member,[100] such deviation shall be deemed authorized in accordance with Rule 8.3. The purpose of this rule is to enable decisions of the Body to become final and not be subject to later challenge due to inadvertent or immaterial non-compliance with the *Rules of Order*.

The purpose of Rule 8.3 is to allow the Presiding Officer and Body to reach decisions and evaluate issues without an unnecessarily strict adherence to the *Rules of Order* and to provide a degree of flexibility to the meeting. The *Rules of Order* is not intended to be the "tail wagging the dog"[101] or for compliance with the rules to become the principal focus of the meeting.

Although Rule 8.3 establishes that most deviations without objection shall not undermine the finality of a decision, certain deviations are material or substantial in nature and may undermine the validity of a decision. These include:

+ The Body's failure to abide by the required vote for a motion (e.g., majority or supermajority). Rule 7.6.

+ The prohibition against proxy or absentee voting. Rule 7.2.

Rule 8.3 does not supersede the right of the Body to entertain a Motion to Reconsider as authorized by the *Rules of Order*. See Section 19.0. The Motion to Reconsider can enable the Body to reopen a decision and correct a material or substantial deficiency by rendering a new decision conforming to the *Rules of Order*.

CHAPTER 4

CLASS & PRIORITY OF POINTS AND MOTIONS

9.0   Class & Priority for Points and Motions

There are three classes[102] for motions and points:

Privileged

Main

Subordinate

Class determines the priority or importance of the motion or point and therefore determines whether the motion or point is "in order" when made, i.e., if the offered motion or point is appropriate for the Body to consider at the time it is presented.

Privileged Motions and Points

Privileged motions, as well as all three points, do not relate to a pending motion. Privileged motions and the points may be raised at any time, are not debatable, and involve an aspect of the meeting that needs to be resolved independent of the business that is then pending before the Body. Privileged *points* do not require the Floor; privileged *motions* require the Floor. The following points and motions are recognized as privileged:

+ Point of Order

+ Point of Information

+ Point of Appeal

+ Motion to Recess

+ Motion for Executive Session

Main Motions

A main motion formally presents a proposition or question to the Body for action. A main motion can be made only when no other motion or point is pending. If a main motion is presented when another motion or point is pending before the Body, the proposed main motion is out of order.

The Body's primary or principal business motion, which is a main motion, is titled by *Bob's Rules* as a "Principal Motion." Together with the Principal Motion, there are four other main motions recognized by *Bob's Rules* that are commonly used in local government decision making. Unlike a Principal Motion, which can propose to the Body a virtually unlimited number of different subjects or topics for action, the other main motions focus the Body's attention on a specific action.

Altogether, the main motions include:

✦ Principal Motion

✦ Motion to Continue or Postpone (when no other main motion is pending)[103]

✦ Motion to Reconsider

✦ Motion to Adjourn

Pursuant to Rule 14.1, a main motion is only in order when no other motion is pending before the Body. Therefore, only one main motion may be on the Floor at any one time.

Subordinate Motions

A subordinate motion is related to and supplements or builds upon a pending main motion. As the name implies, this class of motion is "subordinate" or secondary to a main motion. The Body must address a proposed subordinate motion before a vote on the pending main motion. Once a subordinate motion receives a second and is on the Floor, neither the pending main motion to which the subordinate motion relates nor another subordinate motion is in order.

There are three recognized subordinate motions:

+ Motion to Amend

+ Motion to Continue or Postpone a Matter (when a main motion is pending)[104]

+ Motion to Close Debate

CHAPTER 5

THE POINTS

10.0 Points Generally

Points are a special form of action available to address procedural deficiencies and critical or urgent questions or to challenge the Presiding Officer's decision in the conduct of the meeting. A point requires immediate resolution in order to maintain meeting efficiency. The point presents to the Body a matter of some urgency.

There are three points, which are each recognized and explained in Sections 11.0, 12.0, and 13.0:

+ Point of Order

+ Point of Information

+ Point of Appeal

Rule 10.1

A point may be raised at any time.

Commentary

Because the points are matters of some urgency, points are privileged and are in order at any time. A point is temporarily more important than the matter on the Floor. Any disruption of the present discussion or debate resulting from a point is outweighed by the need for a resolution of the issue underlying the point.

Rule 10.2

A point does not require the Floor.

Commentary

An important aspect of a point is that it does not require the Member to request the Floor. A point is therefore an exception to Rule 4.1.

A Member offering a point may also interrupt another Member who has the Floor. Upon the verbal declaration of a point, the Member temporarily assumes the Floor for the limited purpose of stating the need for the point. The purpose of Rule 10.2 is efficiency. If a Member must await the opportunity to reach the Floor to raise a point, then the resolution of the error, the receipt of the needed information, or the demand for an appeal may come after the Body has devoted time to an inappropriate course of action.

Notwithstanding that a point does not require the Floor, it is a common courtesy when raising a point to await a break in the discussion or debate to limit any unnecessary disruption of the meeting or a speaker. Upon the declaration, the Presiding Officer shall ask any Member with the Floor to hold further comment, invite the Member declaring the point to clarify the issue of urgency, and then take appropriate action to resolve the point.

Rule 10.3

A point does not require a second.

Commentary

A point is not a motion and is not subject to Rule 5.3, which requires that all motions receive a second before the Presiding Officer may acknowledge a motion as properly on the Floor. The reason for this rule is efficiency. A point is simply an expression by a Member that a matter of urgency requires resolution and should be promptly entertained by the Presiding Officer. The consent or approval of another Member is not needed to present a point.

11.0 Point of Order

Purpose

A Point of Order allows any member to call into question the Body's actions regarding compliance with the rules of order.

Requirements and Limitations

Type of Action	Point of Order
When in Order?	At any time
Floor Required?	No
Second Required?	No
Debatable?	No
Subject to Motion to Amend?	No
Friendly Amendment Possible?	No
Vote Required?	No
Subject to Motion to Reconsider?	No

Commentary

A Point of Order (or to "raise a question of order" as it is sometimes expressed) is an opportunity for a Member to question whether the rules or procedures of the Body are being properly followed. The appropriate means of asserting the point is for the Member to await a break in the immediate discussion or debate and state, "Point of Order," and to then wait to be recognized by the Presiding Officer. Upon the Presiding Officer's recognition of the Point of Order, the Presiding Officer shall ask the Member to succinctly state the rule or procedure believed to be violated. A Point of Order does not require a second, is not debatable, is not amendable, and cannot be reconsidered.

The Point in Practice

As an example of a Point of Order, the Body's dialogue might include the following exchange:

Background:	Member A was granted the Floor and proposed a Principal Motion to approve a site plan for a new residential development. She begins to offer her reasons for the motion and engage in debate.
Member B:	"Point of Order."
Presiding Officer:	"Member A, excuse me a moment. Member B, what is your Point of Order?"
Member B:	"I believe we just started to debate a motion that did not receive a second. This is out of order because a motion requires a second before the motion may be on the Floor for debate."
Presiding Officer:	"You are correct, Member B, a second was not offered on the motion. Let us cease debate. Do I hear a second on the motion?"

[A second is offered.]

"We now have a proper motion that received a second. Member A, because you proposed the motion, you have the first right to the Floor and may continue your debate on the motion if you wish."

12.0 Point of Information

Purpose

A Point of Information[105] allows a Member to ask for and *receive* information about a specific matter that is urgent to the Member or to the Body. The need for information typically concerns meeting process or conduct, the clarification of a fact, or other informational matter that is best addressed in the moment and that cannot await an opportunity for the Member to obtain the Floor during discussion or debate. A simple example of the need for information may be to request that the temperature be increased in the meeting room. A more complex request may be to ask for clarification of conflicting testimony offered during a hearing.

Requirements and Limitations

Type of Action	Point of Information
When in Order?	At any time
Floor Required?	No
Second Required?	No
Debatable?	No
Subject to Motion to Amend?	No
Friendly Amendment Possible?	No
Vote Required?	No
Subject to Motion to Reconsider?	No

Commentary

A Point of Information is a request to receive *information*. A Point of Information is not an opportunity for a member to provide information to the Body. A Member's use of a Point of Information to provide information to the Body is out of order.

The Point in Practice

As an example of the proper use of a Point of Information, the Body's dialogue might include the following exchange:

Background:	The Body is engaged in discussion about traffic-calming strategies for a specific neighborhood. Member A has the Floor and offers his thoughts about the concerns raised by the neighborhood's residents.
Member B:	"Point of Information"
Presiding Officer:	"Excuse me a moment, Member A. Member B, what is your Point of Information?"
Member B:	"Member A said there are more than 5,000 vehicles passing through the intersection of Main Street and First Avenue during the peak rush hours. But I recall that our Traffic Engineer stated earlier in her presentation that the traffic count at that intersection during peak hours was at most only 1,500 vehicles. What is the correct number?"
Presiding Officer:	"Let's have the Traffic Engineer provide us the accurate figure for the traffic count."

[The Traffic Engineer provides an answer to the Point of Information as to the correct number of vehicles at peak hours.]

Presiding Officer: "Thank you for clarifying the information, Member B. Member A has the Floor and he may continue with his discussion."

Continuing the example above to illustrate an inappropriate use of a Point of Information, Member A engages in his discussion of traffic-calming improvements to address residents' concerns:

Member B: "Point of Information."

Presiding Officer: "Excuse me a moment, Member A. Member B, what is your Point of Information?"

Member B: "I would like to point out that for the last five years we have experienced rather excessive traffic at this intersection. I suggest that we consider a one-way street as a means of addressing the problem. Further, I believe that…"

Presiding Officer: "Sorry for the interruption, Member B, but I must call you to order. A Point of Information is only available to obtain information necessary to ensure meeting efficiency. You are attempting to provide information to the Body. For that, you need to first have the Floor, which will be provided to you during the course of this discussion. Thank you. Member A, you may continue your discussion."

13.0 Point of Appeal

Purpose

A Point of Appeal provides a Member an opportunity to challenge a decision of the Presiding Officer concerning the application of the rules of order.

Requirements and Limitations

Type of Action	Point of Appeal
When in Order?	Immediately following a Presiding Officer's decision
Floor Required?	No
Second Required?	No
Debatable?	No, but the Moving Member may make a brief statement of the reason for appeal. The Presiding Officer may briefly reply.
Subject to Motion to Amend?	No
Friendly Amendment Possible?	No
Vote Required?	Majority of quorum
Subject to Motion to Reconsider?	No

Commentary

A Point of Appeal is a request by a Member to challenge a decision of the Presiding Officer concerning the application of the rules of order. A Point of Appeal shall be in order immediately following the Presiding Officer's decision. A Point of Appeal is out of order and unavailable where the Body has relied upon the Presiding Officer's decision and continued and concluded the matter in reliance upon, or in accordance with, the Presiding Officer's decision.

No debate is permitted on a Point of Appeal, although the Member making the Point of Appeal may briefly state the reason for the appeal, and the Presiding Officer may briefly explain the Officer's decision. Unless the Presiding Officer agrees with the appeal, corrects the decision, and brings the Body into conformance with the rules, the appeal should proceed, and a vote of the Body will be needed to decide whether to uphold the Presiding Officer's decision.

As a challenge to the Presiding Officer's decision, the point asks whether the Presiding Officer's decision should be upheld. A majority vote is required to support the Presiding Officer's decision. The Presiding Officer is permitted to vote on the appeal. Upon failure to uphold the Presiding Officer's decision, the decision is overruled or invalidated, and the Presiding Officer and Body then continue in the consideration of the matter. If necessary, a new decision may be offered by the Presiding Officer following the successful appeal.

The Point in Practice

The following exchange is an example of the proper use of a Point of Appeal:

Background:	The Body is engaged in debate on a properly seconded motion. A Member who has the Floor offers a Motion to Close Debate.
Presiding Officer:	"We have on the Floor a Motion to Close Debate, and the motion was seconded. The vote on a Motion to Close Debate is not debatable and will require a majority vote of the quorum."
Member A:	"Point of Appeal."

103

Presiding Officer:	"Member A has raised a Point of Appeal. Member A, what is your appeal and the brief reason for the appeal?"
Member A:	"I appeal the Presiding Officer's decision regarding the required vote on a Motion to Close Debate. A Motion to Close Debate requires a two-thirds vote pursuant to our rules of order."
Presiding Officer:	"I believe that closing debate is a rather simple matter only requiring a majority vote like nearly all of our motions.
	"We shall now vote on the appeal. Member A appeals my decision that a vote on a Motion to Close Debate requires a simple majority of this quorum. The question we are now voting on is 'Shall the decision of the Presiding Officer be upheld—that is, am I correct in my decision?' A Point of Appeal requires a majority vote. Will the clerk please call for the vote?"
	[The motion receives one "yes" vote and six "no" votes on the appeal and therefore fails to uphold the Presiding Officer's decision.]
Presiding Officer:	"My decision is overturned on appeal. In looking at our *Rules of Order*, I stand corrected. I will now declare that the Motion to Close Debate will require a vote of two-thirds of the members of the Body. I will thank Member A for correcting my error. Unless we have an appeal of my decision now requiring a two-thirds vote, let us proceed to the vote on the Motion to Close Debate."

In the preceding example, the Presiding Officer could forgo the process of formal voting on the appeal and instead recognize the error in the proceedings and correct the error:

Background: Member A poses the Point of Appeal and the challenge to the Presiding Officer's decision concerning the required vote for a Motion to Close Debate.

Presiding Officer: "Member A appeals my decision regarding the required vote.

                     "Please give me an opportunity to look at the *Rules of Order*. I invite our Town Attorney or the Town Clerk to also offer an opinion on this matter."

Presiding Officer: "Thank you for indulging my brief break. I have reviewed the *Rules of Order*, and I stand corrected. The vote on a Motion to Close Debate is a two-thirds majority.

                     "Member A, thank you for that Point of Appeal, and I will consider the Point of Appeal resolved. We can now proceed to vote on the Motion to Close Debate."

CHAPTER 6

THE MOTIONS

14.0 Motions Generally

A motion is a means to formally ask the Body to take action. All motions are subject to procedural rules to ensure that each motion is made in a timely manner and that the motion is in a form sufficient to enable the Body to render a definitive decision.

All efficient deliberative bodies use motions. All published handbooks offering procedural meeting rules identify numerous motions available to conduct a wide variety of different business and procedural actions. However, it is the specific purpose and particular duties of a Body that best determine the necessary or needed motions. For the purpose and duties of nearly all Colorado local government councils, boards, commissions, and committees—other than perhaps a few of the largest—the necessary or needed motions to conduct local government business include only:

+ Principal Motion   Section 15.0

+ Motion to Continue or Postpone   Section 16.0

+ Motion to Amend   Section 17.0

+ Motion to Close Debate   Section 18.0

+ Motion to Reconsider   Section 19.0

+ Motion to Recess   Section 20.0

+ Motion to Adjourn   Section 21.0

+ Motion for an Executive Session   Section 22.0

Rule 14.1

A main motion is only in order when no other motion is on the Floor.

Commentary

A main motion offers to the Body a general proposition for consideration and debate. Main motions rank lowest in priority, and a main motion is therefore only in order when no other motion is pending before the Body.

The four main motions, which each propose the taking of a general action by the Body, are:

+ Principal Motion (a principal business action)

+ Motion to Continue or Postpone (when no other main motion is pending)[106]

+ Motion to Reconsider

+ Motion to Adjourn

Because a main motion proposes an action that is unrelated to any existing business before the Body, Rule 14.1 advances efficiency by ensuring that the Body is not presently engaged in debate on any other motion. It would be inefficient for the Body—while engaged in debate on another motion—to turn its attention to a new and different proposition and to essentially "juggle" debate on two or more motions.

Rule 14.1 is limited to the presentation of a main motion. Note that, following a main motion being placed on the Floor, subordinate or privileged motions may arise that will relate to the main motion or to a matter that will affect the consideration of the main motion.

Rule 14.2

A debatable motion may be amended by either:

+ A Motion to Amend; or

+ A Friendly Amendment pursuant to Rule 6.1.

Commentary

Rule 14.2 primarily recognizes that only *debatable*[107] motions may be amended.

Some motions propose a singular, defined, and limited request or proposition. Being comprehensive and complete, these types of motions do not lend themselves to debate and are nondebatable.[108] Any modification or amendment of the nondebatable motions would likely contravene the singular purpose of the motion. As an example, a Motion to Close Debate presents only one proposition, which is to close debate. Any attempt to amend a Motion to Close Debate would likely defeat its limited and specific purpose of closing debate. Nondebatable motions proceed directly to a vote of the Body.

Other motions are not singular in purpose, are less refined, and may not completely detail a decision that will be suitable for the required vote of the Body. Such motions therefore present an opportunity for the Body to debate. Debate can often inform the Body that an amendment can clarify, expand, limit, or otherwise modify the motion to meet the needs of the Body. For example, a Motion to Continue or Postpone is debatable, and, during debate, a Member may advocate that the matter need not be continued, or the Member may seek to modify the motion by proposing a different date for the proposed continuation or postponement. A Principal Motion, which is the general business motion, is often broadly stated and may not always include the specificity needed to satisfy other Members of the Body. Principal Motions are debatable and present the most common need for amendment. Amendment of the Principal Motion is often necessary to limit or tailor the motion's purpose, to address the Body's concerns, and to ensure that the motion can receive a fair opportunity for consideration and for a potential majority vote.

As to debatable motions, the two means to amend the motion are a formal Motion to Amend (Section 17.0) and the Friendly Amendment (Rule 6.1).

Rule 14.3
Only one Motion to Amend may be on the Floor at any one time.

Commentary

Motions to Amend are exceedingly common and are often appropriate to tailor a pending main motion into a form acceptable to the Body. At the same time, no meeting practice is more fraught with the potential for confusion than a Motion to Amend.

Most Motions to Amend are straightforward and present little problem for the Body. For example, assume a Principal Motion (a main motion) is offered to approve a land-development application for a new apartment complex. A Motion to Amend (a subordinate motion) is then proposed that will amend the Principal Motion. The amending motion would "require the developer to install a landscape buffer of seven coniferous trees, each a minimum of five feet in height, spaced at least 12 feet apart from one another, and located within a strip between 10 and 20 feet along the west property line in order to protect the adjacent residential property from noise and headlight impacts." Although this Motion to Amend may appear complex based on the number of words in the motion and the references to numbers, heights, and distances, it can be easily understood by the Body because it is a single motion dealing with a single issue of buffering the development with measurable requirements. Once this Motion to Amend is approved, the Principal Motion will stand as amended, and a vote may be taken on the motion as amended.

Following the conclusion of this amendment, one or more other amendments may be proposed and the Motions to Amend handled, one at a time, until the Body is satisfied with the form of the Principal Motion, and it can then proceed to vote on the motion as amended.

Confusion can arise, however, when multiple Motions to Amend are offered and are pending at the same time. This is particularly true where the first Motion to Amend proposes to modify the main motion, the second Motion to Amend proposes to further modify the first motion as it would be amended (that is, the second amendment contemplates that the first amendment will be approved), and the Body engages in debate that includes comments advocating both for and against one or both of the offered amendments. Further, if the motions contain details, numbers, heights, and distances, it can readily be observed that the meeting efficiency will best be served by limiting the number of Motions to Amend placed before the Body at any one time.

In the interest of limiting confusion and creating greater efficiency, *Bob's Rules of Order* prohibits the offering of more than one Motion to Amend at any one time. Under this rule, a single Motion to Amend is in order and will be dispensed with by vote or withdrawal prior to the offering of another Motion to Amend.

Given the limited scope and straightforward nature of local government decisions, limiting the number of Motions to Amend to one at a time presents little, if any, problem. Most matters that are addressed by local government are not sufficiently complex as to require multiple amendments of the main motion. And experience proves that the offering of multiple Motions to Amend is infrequent, if not rare, for most local government matters. On the off chance that multiple Motions to Amend are necessary, the Presiding Officer or the Body can suspend Rule 14.3 on a case-by-case basis. See Rules 8.1 and 8.2.

15.0 Principal Motion

Purpose

The *Rules of Order* recognizes the *Principal Motion*[109] as the title of a main motion that presents a general proposition or a request that the Body take an action. The Principal Motion is intended to address any action other than the actions described in the other seven motions authorized by the *Rules*.

Requirements and Limitations

Type of Action	Main motion
When in Order?	When no motion is pending
Floor Required?	Yes
Second Required?	Yes
Debatable?	Yes
Subject to Motion to Amend?	Yes
Friendly Amendment Possible?	Yes

Vote Required?	Ordinarily, a majority of the quorum, but some motions will require a supermajority vote. Consult with legal counsel.
Subject to Motion to Reconsider?	Yes

Commentary

There are as many Principal Motions as there are subject matters that the Body may consider. To be in order, a Principal Motion must state an affirmative or positive proposition or question. See Rule 5.2.

Regarding the vote required for a Principal Motion, the vast majority of these motions will be subject to the common rule that requires a majority of a quorum for approval. See Rule 7.6.

However, for Colorado local government, special statutory voting requirements may also be imposed that will require a Principal Motion to meet a different voting requirement. The local government attorney should be consulted regarding the special voting requirements of state and local law and whether the requirements are applicable to the Principal Motion before the Body. By way of just two examples:

+ A *municipality's* Principal Motion to adopt an emergency ordinance requires a vote of three-fourths (3/4) of the members of the governing body of the municipality.[110]

+ Colorado state law requires a two-thirds (2/3) vote of all the Members of the governing body of a *municipality* to approve a change in zoning or zoning regulations in the event of a properly filed protest.[111]

16.0 Motion to Continue or Postpone

+ To a Future Day and Time

+ To an Uncertain Time

+ Indefinitely

Purpose

The purpose of a Motion to Continue or Postpone[112] is to defer or delay consideration of an agenda item. The deferral or delay may take the form of three different options related to time described in this section.

Requirements and Limitations

Type of Action	■ *Main* motion when no other motion is pending
	■ *Subordinate* motion when a Principal Motion is pending
When in Order?	Only when no motion or only a Principal Motion is pending
Floor Required?	Yes
Second Required?	Yes
Debatable?	Yes
Subject to Motion to Amend?	No
Friendly Amendment Possible?	No
Vote Required?	Majority of quorum
Subject to Motion to Reconsider?	Yes

Commentary

The Motion to Continue or Postpone is an effective and necessary tool for local government meetings. The Body may wish to postpone a scheduled agenda item that is not yet before the Body for a variety of reasons, such as lacking sufficient time for a full consideration of the item or the absence of the applicant or a key staff member. For an agenda item that is open and before the Body, the Body may learn during discussion or debate that certain information is needed for a decision, and a continuation of the item will allow the information to be assembled and presented to the Body at a later date.

A Motion to Continue or Postpone an agenda item is available regardless of whether the item is not yet pending before the Body or the item is open[113] and under consideration. Using the term "continue," "postpone," "delay," or some other expression in the motion is not important as long as the clear intent of the motion is to delay the matter to a specified date and time, to an uncertain date and time, or indefinitely as referenced in the motion.

The Motion to Continue or Postpone is a hybrid motion, meaning it can serve as a main motion or as a subordinate motion. The motion is available as a main motion when it is used to continue a matter when no motion is on the Floor. The motion is available as a subordinate motion when a Principal Motion is on the Floor and before the Body.[114]

A Motion to Continue or Postpone is not in order when a privileged motion (such as a Motion to Recess) or a subordinate motion (such as a Motion to Amend) is on the Floor. Resolution of all privileged and subordinate motions is necessary before offering a Motion to Continue or Postpone.

A Motion to Continue or Postpone should be used as a *main motion* whenever possible—that is, when no other *motion* is pending before the Body. Continuing or postponing a matter when a Principal Motion is on the Floor, although permitted, can create some complexity for the local government meeting. In the event that a Principal Motion is on the Floor, the continuation or postponement of the agenda item will carry forward the pending Principal Motion to the future meeting. However, a local government, at its finest, is often challenged to accurately recall and restate a motion that was pending during a meeting just a few weeks prior, let alone accurately recall a motion that was on the Floor several months or a year ago. But when offered as a main motion, the Motion to Continue or Postpone will allow the Body to take up the matter knowing that no motion was pending on the Floor from the previous meeting.

The Motion to Continue or Postpone requires a decision from the Moving Member regarding the proposed duration of the continuation from among three options:

+ To a future day and time
+ To an uncertain time
+ Indefinitely

To a Future Day and Time

The Motion to Continue or Postpone an agenda item may be stated as a continuation or postponement to a *specific* future date and time.

The motion will require that the Moving Member identify the specific date and time for the agenda item to be returned to the Body. The Body's legal counsel may also recommend that the location (place) where the continued or postponed matter will be heard be included in the motion, especially when the Body uses multiple locations for meetings, may alternate between in-person and virtual meetings, or specifically when the matter is quasi-judicial in nature and notice is of significant importance to ensure fairness.[115]

To an Uncertain Time

The Motion to Continue or Postpone an agenda item may be stated *without* a specific time for the matter to be returned to the Body. This motion is not a Motion to Continue or Postpone indefinitely (see below). Instead, the motion *requires* the agenda item to be returned to the Body, but the date of the return cannot be established with any certainty. A common reason for such a motion would be that the setting of the agenda item on a future agenda requires an evaluation of other items to come before the Body on future agendas that may be of more urgency or importance. Additionally, it may be necessary to coordinate the attendance of necessary staff members or consultants at the future meeting. Continuing or postponing to an uncertain time can provide the manager or administrator the flexibility of returning the agenda item to the Body as time and resources permit. As with continuing or postponing to a future date and time, it may be necessary to republish or repost notice of the continued matter and the meeting date, time, and place once the meeting date is determined.

Indefinitely

A Body may need to remove an item from the agenda or cease consideration of an open agenda item with the understanding that the item will not be returned or reintroduced to the Body in the future. This need may be based upon the fact that the matter is no longer a concern for the local government or that the Body anticipates there is insufficient interest or support to devote any amount of time to the consideration of the agenda item. A successful Motion to Continue or Postpone *indefinitely* will effectively remove the item from the agenda and also direct that the item will not be rescheduled for later consideration. A Motion to Continue or Postpone indefinitely will not prevent the Body from taking up the topic in the future, although the setting of a new agenda item would be necessary to bring the topic back before the Body.

As an important caution, a Motion to Continue or Postpone indefinitely is not advisable where the item involves a quasi-judicial matter. Recall that, for quasi-judicial matters, the applicant has a legal right to a hearing, the opportunity to be heard, and a right to a final decision of the government.[116] Indefinitely postponing an agenda item may appear to deprive the applicant of the right to be heard and a decision. Legal counsel should be consulted regarding the use of this motion for any quasi-judicial matter and, more appropriately, to consider the use of a Motion to Continue or Postpone to a future day and time or to an uncertain time, which motion expresses a direction that the quasi-judicial matter will be heard and decided in the future.

The Motion in Practice

As an example of a Motion to Continue or Postpone an agenda item to a future date and time, the motion may be stated as:

"I move to continue Agenda Item 13(b), which is a discussion of County Property Tax Revenue Projections, to April 16, 2026, at 4:00 p.m. here in the Commissioner's Board Room."

As an example of a Motion to Continue or Postpone an agenda item that is open and under discussion or debate to an uncertain time, the motion might be stated as:

"I agree with the proposal before us to adjust the fees for the Center Park Swimming Pool, but I believe we need more information on the actual number of visits we experienced over the last five years. Whether the visits are increasing or decreasing is relevant in my decision to set new fees. We need to give the City Manager time to assemble the data and to find time on a future agenda for us to continue this discussion. I move to continue this discussion of the fees to be charged next year for the use of the Center Park Swimming Pool to an uncertain date and time."

As an example of a Motion to Continue or Postpone an agenda item indefinitely, the motion might be stated as:

"I move to postpone indefinitely Ordinance Number 22, which would require all cats in the town be kept on a leash."

17.0 Motion to Amend

Purpose

The purpose of a Motion to Amend is to modify a *debatable* motion on the Floor.

Requirements and Limitations

Type of Action	Subordinate motion (to a debatable motion)
When in Order?	When a *debatable* motion is on the Floor
Floor Required?	Yes
Second Required?	Yes
Debatable?	Yes
Subject to Motion to Amend?	No
Friendly Amendment Possible?	No
Vote Required?	Majority of quorum
Subject to Motion to Reconsider?	No

Commentary

A Motion to Amend is available and applicable only to a debatable motion on the Floor. The motion must provide specificity as to the intended amendment of the debatable motion. See Rule 5.2.

To advance the efficiency of a meeting, Rule 14.3 prohibits a second Motion to Amend when a Motion to Amend is already on the Floor.

The Motion in Practice

The following dialogue highlights the offer of a Motion to Amend a debatable motion.

Background:	The Body is considering Ordinance No. 6, which would create a new municipal offense for an unlicensed animal. The Ordinance provides for a penalty for the first offense of $100. The Body is concluding its discussion of the Ordinance.
Member A:	"I move to approve Ordinance No. 6 as presented to us tonight."
Member B:	"Second."
Presiding Officer:	"We have a proper Principal Motion on the Floor that has received a second to approve Ordinance No. 6. Any discussion?"

[Member C requests the Floor.]

Presiding Officer:	"Yes, Member C, the Floor is yours."
Member C:	"Thank you. I move to amend the motion to change the amount of the penalty for the first violation as stated in section 1-1-3 on page 3 of

Ordinance No. 6 from $100 for the first offense to $200 for the first offense."

Member D: "Second."

Presiding Officer: "We have a Motion to Amend before us to change the penalty in section 1-1-3 of Ordinance No. 6 from $100 to $200 for the first offense. We will debate the Motion to Amend first before we consider the Principal Motion to approve Ordinance No. 6. The Motion to Amend is debatable and requires a simple majority vote. Member C, Rule 5.6 allows you the right to the Floor first to speak to your Motion to Amend."

Member A: "Thank you, but I am fine with the motion I offered."

Presiding Officer: "I see no one else wishing to comment or debate the offered Motion to Amend Ordinance No. 6. The Motion to Amend will make a change in section 1-1-3 of Ordinance No. 6 to set a $200 penalty for the first offense. Would the clerk call for the vote on the Motion to Amend only?"

[Motion receives majority vote of approval.]

Presiding Officer: "The Motion to Amend is approved, so Ordinance No. 6 is now amended to change the penalty for a first offense to $200. We now turn to the Principal Motion to approve Ordinance 6. Any debate on Ordinance No. 6 as amended?"

[The consideration of the Principal Motion to approve Ordinance No. 6 as amended continues.]

18.0 Motion to Close Debate

Purpose

A Motion to Close Debate, which is sometimes confusingly expressed as a "Motion to Call the Question,"[117] will allow the Body to cease debate, which will effectively require an immediate vote on a pending debatable motion.

Requirements and Limitations

Type of Action	Subordinate motion
When in Order?	When a *debatable* motion is on the Floor
Floor Required?	Yes
Second Required?	Yes
Debatable?	No
Subject to Motion to Amend? Friendly Amendment Possible?	No No
Vote Required?	Two-thirds (2/3) of the quorum
Subject to Motion to Reconsider?	No

Commentary

A Motion to Close Debate is a subordinate motion available only while a *debatable* motion is on the Floor. Understandably, the motion is only in order for debatable motions because there is no need to close debate when the motion is not subject to debate. But, very importantly, the motion is not available to stop the Body's discussion when no motion is on the Floor.

The approval of a Motion to Close Debate will require the Presiding Officer to immediately call for the vote on the pending debatable motion.

The Motion to Close Debate is not a debatable motion because the motion presents a single unambiguous proposition—that is, to close debate on the pending debatable motion. Members must vote on the proposition to cease the debate, or, if the vote is unsuccessful, the Body will continue the debate.

Because the motion will deny the Members the right to debate the merits of a pending motion, a supermajority vote of two-thirds (2/3) of the quorum is required. This supermajority is appropriate. Denying the voice of Members can be viewed as antithetical to local government's goals of an open, transparent, and participatory meeting. However, there is a point at which debate becomes stale, arguments repeated, and no new issues are raised concerning the need to approve or reject the pending motion. In these cases, a Motion to Close Debate may be in order.

The Motion in Practice

As an example of a Motion to Close Debate and a Point of Information, the dialogue of the Body might include the following exchange:

Background:	A debatable Principal Motion to approve a land-use application is pending before the Body. The Body is engaged in debate. The Members have actively participated in the debate, and most everyone has expressed their views. The debate is becoming repetitive. Member A has the Floor.
Member A:	"I move to close debate."

Member B:	"Second."
Presiding Officer:	"We have a Motion to Close Debate. If approved, this motion will close any continuing debate on the motion to approve the land-use application that is presently before us. We would then proceed immediately to a vote on the motion to approve. A Motion to Close Debate is not debatable and will require a supermajority of our quorum by a two-thirds vote. Would the clerk please call for the vote?"
Member C:	"Point of Information."
Presiding Officer:	"Let us hold for a moment on the call for the vote. Member C, what is your Point of Information?"
Member C:	"I have not yet offered my concerns about the land-use application. Will I get a chance to speak before we vote?"
Presiding Officer:	"No, if the Motion to Close Debate is successfully approved by a vote of two-thirds of the quorum, no further debate will be allowed, and we will vote on the motion to approve the land-use application."
	[The Motion to Close Debate is approved by the required two-thirds of the quorum.]
Presiding Officer:	"The Motion to Close Debate is approved. No further debate is permitted on the pending Principal Motion to approve the land-use application. I will ask the City Clerk to please call for the vote on the Principal Motion to approve."

19.0 Motion to Reconsider

Purpose

The purpose of a Motion to Reconsider is to effectively negate or vacate a previous decision on a motion of the Body and to return the Body to a point immediately prior to the offer of the previously approved motion. The Motion to Reconsider allows the Body to recommence debate and eventually propose a new motion or action regarding the matter. A Motion to Reconsider does not automatically reverse the prior decision of the Body.

Requirements and Limitations

Type of Action	Main motion
When in Order?	Only when: (1) No motion is pending before the Body; and (2) When made by a Member who voted on the prevailing side of the decision to be reconsidered; and (a) at the same meeting at which the decision to be reconsidered was approved; or (b) at the *next regular meeting* of the Body at which the decision to be reconsidered was approved.
Floor Required?	Yes
Second Required?	Yes

Debatable?	Yes, but only as to the reasons to support the reconsideration. No debate of the original decision is allowed.
Subject to Motion to Amend?	No
Friendly Amendment Possible?	No
Vote Required?	Two-thirds (2/3) of the quorum

Commentary

A Motion to Reconsider is an extraordinary motion that requires a degree of care when presenting and, if approved, care in processing the matter to be reconsidered. A successful Motion to Reconsider will effectively negate or vacate the vote on a previously decided motion and cause the matter to be reopened for reconsideration, and another motion to approve or reject the matter would be in order at the time of reconsideration.

Due to the potential effect of a Motion to Reconsider on a previously rendered decision of the Body and the legal rights of interested parties, it is strongly recommended that the Body's legal counsel be consulted regarding any proposal to offer a Motion to Reconsider. This is especially true for quasi-judicial[118] decisions.

Very importantly, a Motion to Reconsider is only in order at the same meeting at which the decision to be reconsidered was made or at the *next* regular meeting of the Body. The reason for this requirement is that a decision of the Body must become final with some promptness so that actions can be taken to implement the decision. For example, the approval of a construction contract will require the execution of the contract by the contractor and the government. Once the contract is executed and the construction project is underway, the potential reversal of the approval of the construction contract could potentially expose the government to a claim for breach of contract. Limitations on the timing and availability of a Motion for Reconsideration are therefore necessary.

The Motion to Reconsider must be made by a Member who voted with the prevailing majority on the approval of the original motion. The reason for this requirement is that a decision made by a majority of the Body constitutes a decision of the entire Body even though one or more Members voted in the minority. It makes reasonable sense that only a Member who voted affirmatively as part of the prevailing majority should be authorized to seek reconsideration of the majority's decision. A Motion to Reconsider does not provide an opportunity for a voter in the minority of a decision to challenge the majority. A Motion to Reconsider is out of order when offered by a Member of the minority.

The required second on the motion need *not* be made by a Member from the prevailing side. A second is merely offered as the Member's support for the Body to enter debate on the motion or to advance the proposed motion to a vote. See Commentary for Rule 5.3.

The Motion to Reconsider is debatable only for the reasons to explain or justify the need for a reconsideration of a decision. It would be out of order to use a Motion to Reconsider as a means to reengage the debate on the merits of a prior decision. For example, the Member seeking a Motion to Reconsider may assert that the reconsideration is necessary due to further reflection by the Member upon the evidence that was presented during a public hearing or that the Member's subsequent and more detailed review of a contract approved by the Body warrants a new discussion and new vote. The Motion to Reconsider only asks the Body to vacate its prior decision and reopen the matter for additional consideration. If approved, only then would the Body be authorized to engage in the debate on the merits of the original matter.

A supermajority vote of two-thirds (2/3) of the quorum is required for approval. This higher voting standard makes reasonable sense. Permitting a simple majority of a quorum to reopen a previous final decision of the Body can be disruptive to the goal of finality of decision making and, moreover, would potentially subject a greater number of final decisions to be reopened merely when one Member in the majority had a change of heart. The supermajority ensures that strong support exists to warrant reopening a decided matter or issue.

Once a Motion to Reconsider is approved by the required supermajority, the previous decision is negated or vacated, and the matter will be reopened for additional evaluation and consideration. All proceedings, testimony, evidence, and debate on the matter that was presented during the initial consideration of the original matter will remain part of the official record when the matter is reopened; only the decision or vote taken is negated or vacated. In effect, a successful Motion to Reconsider returns the Body to a point prior to the original motion and then leaves the matter undecided until a new motion is offered following reconsideration.

In the event of a successful vote on a Motion to Reconsider, it is recommended that the reconsideration of the original matter be scheduled for a future meeting as opposed to being heard at the same meeting at which the Motion to Reconsider was approved. This recommendation stems from the fact that the matter under reconsideration may oftentimes require new public notice so that interested parties (and especially an applicant in a quasi-judicial matter whose rights are potentially affected by the reconsideration) are apprised of the reconsideration and can attend and participate in the reconsideration. Even when a successful Motion to Reconsider is presented in the same night as the motion subject to reconsideration, the parties present for the original matter and motion may have departed the meeting after what appeared to those attending to be a final decision on the original motion. Fairness, as well as the transparency of government, will often dictate that the reconsideration be scheduled for a future meeting and new notice be provided in a manner consistent with the original matter being reconsidered. Again, due to the extraordinary nature of a Motion to Reconsider and the potential impact on the rights of interested parties, the Body's legal counsel should always be consulted on the use of a Motion to Reconsider and the potential impacts of the action.

Special Note: Reconsideration and Repeal

There are important differences between the reconsideration of a decision and the repeal of a decision. Reconsideration will vacate the previous decision and return the Body to the point immediately prior to the motion and the decision. The offer of a Motion to Reconsider is limited by time (presented only at the same meeting or the next regular meeting of the Body), may only be offered by a Member who voted on the prevailing side of the original motion, and requires a two-thirds (2/3) vote of the quorum for approval.

In contrast, the repeal of a decision will summarily rescind or annul a previous decision. Because a repeal would require a Principal Motion (e.g., "I move to repeal Ordinance 19"), the motion is not limited by time, may be made by any Member, and requires only a majority vote. However, it is critically important that the Body consult with local legal counsel regarding the legal implications associated with any proposed repeal. Some decisions by law are not subject to repeal, some decisions cannot be repealed because irrevocable actions were undertaken in reliance on the decision, and a repeal may undermine the legal rights of the local government and individuals who relied upon the original decision.[119]

The Motion in Practice

As an example of a Motion to Reconsider, the Body's dialogue might involve the following exchange:

Background: No motion is pending. Member A has the Floor.

Member A: "I move to reconsider our decision to approve Ordinance 14, which required all owners to keep their dogs on leashes at all times. Ordinance 14 was approved at our last meeting, and I voted with the majority in approving the Ordinance."

Member B   "Second."

Member C: "Point of Order."

Presiding Officer: "Member C, what is your Point of Order?"

Member C: "Member B was not on the prevailing side of the original vote on the matter. His second is out of order."

Presiding Officer: "Our rules of order provide that a second to a Motion to Reconsider may be offered by any Member. I accept the second.

"On the Floor is a Motion to Reconsider Ordinance 14 concerning our new dog-leash law. The motion was properly seconded. If we approve this Motion to Reconsider, the motion will negate or vacate our prior decision on Ordinance 14 and then require us to reengage in continuing debate on the Ordinance. If approved, any future action on Ordinance 14 will require a new motion and a new vote.

"Member A, did you want to speak to your Motion to Reconsider? Please note that you are free to discuss the reason why you wish to seek reconsideration, but this is not an opportunity to debate the merits of Ordinance 14. If your Motion to Reconsider is successful, we will reopen the debate on the merits of Ordinance 14."

Member A: "Thank you. I would like us to reconsider Ordinance 14 because, upon reflection over the last week, I learned that many communities have alternatives to restricting dogs to a leash, like voice command. I do not think we adequately explored any alternatives. I am proposing that we reopen the matter for more discussion, especially on alternatives to using a leash."

Presiding Officer: "Any other debate concerning whether we should reconsider Ordinance 14? Seeing none, please note that approval of a Motion to Reconsider requires a supermajority of two-thirds of the quorum. I call to the Body's attention that Ordinance 14 was not on our agenda tonight, so, if the Motion to Reconsider is approved, our staff will need to schedule Ordinance 14 on a future agenda. Also, the staff will need to provide or publish any required notices to the public concerning our reconsideration of Ordinance 14. The clerk will call the vote."

[The Motion to Reconsider fails to gain a supermajority vote of two-thirds of the quorum.]

Presiding Officer: "The motion fails. We will now move to the next item on our agenda."

20.0 Motion to Recess

Purpose

The purpose of a Motion to Recess is to provide the Body a temporary break in the meeting.

Requirements and Limitations

Type of Action	Privileged motion
When in Order?	Any time
Floor Required?	Yes
Second Required?	Yes
Debatable?	No
Subject to Motion to Amend?	No
Friendly Amendment Possible?	No
Vote Required?	Majority of quorum
Subject to Motion to Reconsider?	No

Commentary

A recess may be needed for a variety of reasons, including a restroom break, to allow citizens an opportunity to exit the room at the conclusion of an agenda item without disrupting the proceedings, to allow a Member to consult with legal counsel, or to simply reduce the Members' meeting stress during or after a contentious hearing. The motion is privileged and may be offered at any time.

A Motion to Recess is a necessary motion for the Body because it is common that a bylaw provision for the Body appropriately prohibits Members from leaving the meeting room without an approved recess or without the discretionary consent of the Presiding Officer. Additionally, leaving the meeting room during a quasi-judicial hearing can be problematic because Members' continuous presence is needed to hear all the available evidence that will support the decision. An absence from the meeting room can also potentially deprive the meeting of a quorum when the quorum was established with the minimum number of Members.

However, a Motion to Recess is not typically needed because the Presiding Officer will oftentimes use discretion (see Rule 3.4) to declare a recess at appropriate times or between lengthy agenda items. The Presiding Officer can also use discretion to unilaterally call for a recess in response to a Member's Point of Information asking if a recess would be entertained.

Notwithstanding that a formal Motion to Recess may not be commonly needed, the availability of the motion is necessary. The Presiding Officer may desire to push ahead on the agenda, yet a majority of the Body supports taking a break. In such a case, a Motion to Recess is the appropriate means for a majority of Members to defeat the Presiding Officer's direction. And, in such an instance, a formal Motion to Recess is preferable to a Point of Appeal that would challenge the Presiding Officer's decision to not take a recess. A Point of Appeal can be seen as an adversarial move to challenge the Presiding Officer's leadership. In contrast, a Motion to Recess is seen as a more positive approach simply assessing the interests of the Body to take a break.

A Motion to Recess does not require a stated reason for the recess. However, a reason, as well as the duration of break desired, can assist Members in supporting the motion or persuading the Presiding Officer to unilaterally call for a recess.

The Motion in Practice

As an example of a Motion to Recess, the following dialogue highlights the manner in which the motion might arise:

Background:	The Body is debating a Principal Motion to approve the annual budget.
Member A:	"Point of Information."
Presiding Officer:	"Member A, what is your Point of Information?
Member A:	"Would the Presiding Officer entertain a recess for 15 minutes or until 7:30 so I may take care of an important phone call?"
Presiding Officer:	"I am not inclined to call a recess. We have a lengthy agenda, and I would like to adjourn this meeting at a reasonable hour this evening. I expect we will complete this agenda item in ten minutes, and we can entertain a recess at that time."
Member A:	[who requested and was granted the Floor] "Thank you. I move to recess the meeting for 15 minutes and reassemble at 7:30."
Member B:	"Second."
Presiding Officer:	"We have a Motion to Recess until 7:30, and the motion received a second. This motion is not debatable and requires a majority vote of the

Body for approval. The clerk shall call for the vote."

[The Body abides by the result of the vote.]

21.0 Motion to Adjourn

Purpose

The purpose of a Motion to Adjourn is to allow the Body to formally terminate the meeting by vote.

Requirements and Limitations

Type of Action	Main motion
When in Order?	When no motion is pending before the Body
Floor Required?	Yes
Second Required?	Yes
Debatable?	Yes
Subject to Motion to Amend?	No
Friendly Amendment Possible?	No
Vote Required?	Majority of quorum
Subject to Motion to Reconsider?	No

Commentary

Rule 1.6 provides that a meeting cannot conclude without a formal action. Rule 1.6 is necessary to prevent Members of the Body from simply leaving a meeting without taking the necessary actions to properly dispense with or to postpone pending agenda items.[120] In addition, formal adjournment will notify attendees that no further business will be undertaken by the Body.

For most meetings, the Body will conclude all items on the agenda, and the Presiding Officer will unilaterally declare the meeting adjourned. Unilaterally declaring a meeting adjourned is within the discretion of the Presiding Officer (see Rule 3.4). Absent a Point of Appeal to challenge the Presiding Officer's decision to adjourn, the meeting will stand adjourned without need for a formal Motion to Adjourn.[121]

However, in the event a majority of the Body seeks to end the meeting, the Motion to Adjourn is available.

Some procedural rules of order recognize a Motion to Adjourn as a privileged motion. Because a privileged motion is in order at any time, classifying a Motion to Adjourn as privileged would allow a majority of the Body to adjourn and leave the meeting without dispensing with a matter under discussion or debate and without properly postponing upcoming agenda items. Allowing the Body to walk away from pending discussion or debate is problematic in the setting of a local government meeting, particularly during a quasi-judicial hearing.

Bob's Rules of Order recognizes the Motion to Adjourn as a main motion. Categorizing the Motion to Adjourn as a main motion requires that there be no pending motion on the Floor. This prevents the Body from leaving the meeting without addressing pending motions and provides the opportunity for the Body to consider postponing items scheduled on the agenda before entertaining a Motion to Adjourn. The Motion to Adjourn is debatable.

Caution should be exercised when moving to adjourn when agenda items remain pending on the agenda for which required public notice was issued (such as a public-hearing publication or posting of property). Adjourning a meeting that was preceded by published notice of the hearing must be properly continued to a future date by a Motion to Continue or Postpone. Otherwise, an adjournment without a proper postponement may require that new notice be published and/or posted as may be required. The Body's legal counsel should be consulted to ensure that a Motion to Adjourn made before the conclusion of scheduled agenda items is handled in the most efficient manner.

A Motion to Adjourn is not subject to a Motion to Amend or a Friendly Amendment. Proposed amendments almost invariably pertain to delaying the adjournment to a time following the handling of an open or an upcoming item on the agenda. For example, a Member may propose to amend the Motion to Adjourn to state that it will be "effective upon the conclusion of the current agenda item." Such an amendment is unnecessary and cumbersome in the sense that the Motion to Adjourn would be timely and most appropriate when the current agenda item is concluded.

The Motion in Practice

As an example of a Motion to Adjourn at the conclusion of the meeting agenda, such motion in practice might follow the following discussion:

Presiding Officer:	"We have reached the end of our agenda, but I have three matters I would like to discuss with the Board of Trustees."
Member A:	[requests and is provided the Floor] "It is now 10:00 p.m. and we have addressed all the items on our agenda. I move to adjourn this meeting."
Member B:	"Second."
Presiding Officer:	"A Motion to Adjourn is debatable. Does anyone wish to speak to the motion? Seeing none, would the clerk please call the vote?"

[A majority of the quorum votes to approve the motion.]

Presiding Officer: "This meeting is adjourned. Thank you."

As an example of a Motion to Adjourn where the agenda includes items remaining to be addressed, the dialogue may include:

Background: No motion is pending, and Member A has the Floor.

Member A: "I move to adjourn."

Member B: "Second."

Presiding Officer: "Before I acknowledge the Motion to Adjourn, I will pose a Point of Information.[122] I ask the Town Attorney to advise us on the effect of the proposed adjournment when we have agenda items pending and one is a public hearing. Will the Town Attorney provide an opinion on what steps we need to take before adjourning?"

Body's Attorney: "We have three items remaining on the agenda, and one is a public hearing for which special notice was published. If the Body adjourns without properly postponing the public hearing to a specific date, time, and place, we will need to publish new notice. So, there are several different processes available:

"First, we need to resolve the Motion to Adjourn. Because it is a main motion, we are unable to entertain a Motion to Postpone because it also is a main motion and requires that no other motion be on the Floor.

"One option is for the Presiding Officer to ask Member A to withdraw the Motion to Adjourn because it is not yet on the Floor.[123]

"Another option is for the Presiding Officer to acknowledge the Motion to Adjourn as properly on the Floor and then propose a Friendly Withdrawal of the motion.

"If a voluntary withdrawal or a Friendly Withdrawal cannot be achieved, the Body will need to vote on the Motion to Adjourn.

"If the motion is either withdrawn or rejected by a vote, the Body can then entertain a Motion to Postpone the public hearing and all other agenda items to our next scheduled meeting. Once everything is properly postponed to a specific date, the Body can entertain a new Motion to Adjourn.

"Obviously, if a majority of the Body does not wish to adjourn and instead desires to continue the meeting, any proposed Motion to Postpone will fail."

Presiding Officer: "Thank you. I will ask Member A to withdraw the Motion to Adjourn since it is not yet on the Floor."

Member A: "I will withdraw the Motion to Adjourn."

Presiding Officer: "Thank you, Member A. I will move to postpone[124] all items remaining on our agenda, and I will specifically mention Item 9, which is a public hearing on an application to rezone the Pedersen

Property, to our next regular meeting, which is December 8, 2026, at 6:30 p.m. here in the City Council Chambers at 123 Main Street.

"I will speak to my motion. If you are inclined to have us adjourn the meeting at this time, I would suggest you vote to approve the Motion to Postpone. If the motion is successful with a majority vote, then no items will remain on the agenda, and I can declare the meeting adjourned without the need for a formal motion. Would anyone wish to debate the Motion to Postpone? Seeing none, I will call for the vote."

[The Motion to Postpone is approved by a majority vote.]

Presiding Officer: "The Motion to Postpone is approved. Because we have no further business on our agenda, I will declare this meeting adjourned."

CHAPTER 7

EXECUTIVE SESSION

22.0 Motion for an Executive Session

Purpose

The purpose of a Motion for an Executive Session is to take advantage of the statutorily authorized privilege of convening in a confidential meeting for the discussion of limited matters authorized by the Colorado Open Meetings Law, C.R.S. § 24-6-402(4).

Requirements and Limitations

Type of Action	Privileged motion
When in Order?	Any time
Floor Required?	Yes
Second Required?	Yes
Debatable?	No
Subject to Motion to Amend?	No
Friendly Amendment Possible?	No
Vote Required?	Two-thirds (2/3) of the quorum
Subject to Motion to Reconsider?	No

Commentary

Executive sessions are expressly permitted by state law to allow the Body to discuss certain topics in a closed non-public and confidential setting. State law recognizes that the public disclosure of certain confidential information may harm the public interest, impair the rights of employees, undermine the security of the public, or place the government at a disadvantage in negotiations and in potential or ongoing litigation matters.

The Motion for an Executive Session is perhaps the most challenging of motions. The motion requires careful consideration and oftentimes advance preparation of the motion's language. This is necessary in order to meet the statutory mandate that the motion include (a) a citation to the specific statutory subsection of the Colorado Revised Statutes which authorizes the session[125] and (b) identification of the particular matter to be discussed in as much detail as possible without compromising the purpose of the executive session.[126] Local charters, ordinances, and policies may also impose additional limitations and requirements on the Body's ability to hold an executive session.

Before acknowledging a Motion for Executive Session in accordance with Rule 5.4, the Presiding Officer should carefully consider whether the form of the motion meets the requirements for a Motion for an Executive Session. It is a wise practice to prepare the motion in advance of the meeting with the assistance of local legal counsel or to confirm with legal counsel during the meeting that a proposed motion is satisfactory.

Errors in the form of the motion *may* result in any confidential information discussed in the session becoming subject to public disclosure, and this disclosure may harm the government's interests. It is strongly advised that legal counsel be consulted on the form and language of the motion and that a script or checklist be prepared to help ensure all required procedures are followed.

The most common types of executive sessions for Colorado local government that are authorized by the Colorado Open Meetings Law[127] include the following sessions:

(a) Purchase, acquisition, lease, transfer, or sale of any real, personal, or other property interest—except that no executive session shall be held for the purpose of concealing the fact that a Member of the local public Body has a personal interest in such purchase, acquisition, lease, transfer, or sale.[128]

(b) Conferences with an attorney for the local public Body for the purposes of receiving legal advice on specific legal questions. The mere presence or participation of an attorney at an executive session of the local public Body is not sufficient to qualify the executive session as a session involving legal advice.[129]

(c) Matters required to be kept confidential by federal or state law or rules and regulations. The Body shall announce the specific citation of the statutes or rules that are the basis for such confidentiality before holding the executive session.[130]

(d) Specialized details of security arrangements or investigations, including defenses against terrorism, both domestic and foreign, and including where disclosure of the matters discussed might reveal information that could be used for the purpose of committing, or avoiding prosecution for, a violation of the law.[131]

(e) Determining positions relative to matters that may be subject to negotiations, developing strategy for negotiations, and instructing negotiators.[132]

(f) Personnel matters except if the employee who is the subject of the session has requested an open meeting or if the personnel matter involves more than one employee and all of the employees have requested an open meeting.[133] However, an executive session cannot be held to discuss:

  (i) an elected official or an appointed Member of the Body;[134] or (ii)　the appointment of a person to fill an appointed[135] or elective office; or

(iii)　personnel policies that do not require the discussion of matters personal to particular employees.[136]

(g)　Consideration of any documents protected by the mandatory nondisclosure provisions of the Colorado Open Records Act[137]— except that all consideration of documents or records that are work product as defined in C.R.S. § 24-72-202 or that are subject to the governmental or deliberative process privilege shall occur in a public meeting unless an executive session is otherwise allowed pursuant to state law.

Again, local charters, ordinances, and policies may limit the availability of these executive sessions or impose additional limitations and requirements on the Body's ability to hold an executive session. While other executive session purposes are authorized by state law, they may be less common or not applicable for local government.

The *Rules of Order* does not permit debate on the Motion for an Executive Session. The purpose of this limitation on debate is to avoid the potential disclosure of confidential information. If debate were permitted, it would often be challenging to publicly identify "why" the executive session is needed without risking disclosure by a Member of confidential information. Because, in practice, the need for an executive session and its justifications are typically vetted and established by legal and administrative staff before the meeting and the purpose for the executive session is generally known to the Presiding Officer (and often the Members), executive session motions do not commonly receive questions from the Body. As a result, a blanket prohibition on debate is reasonable. In a rare instance when a Member is uncertain about the reason for an executive session, a request to the Presiding Officer to call a recess may be in order to allow the Member to consult with the Presiding Officer, administrative staff, or the Body's legal counsel.

Critically important is that a supermajority of two-thirds of the quorum is required for approval of an executive session motion pursuant to the Colorado Open Meetings Law. An error in the vote may result in the content and discussion of the executive session becoming public[138] and the award of court costs and reasonable attorney's fees.[139]

Confusion sometimes arises upon the effect of a failure of the Motion for Executive Session to receive the necessary vote. A Motion for Executive Session is a proposal to enter a non-public setting to discuss a limited and statutorily authorized subject or topic. The failure of the motion to secure the necessary two-thirds vote of a quorum merely rejects the requested opportunity to hold the discussion in a non-public setting. The motion's rejection does not mandate that the local government discuss the subject or topic in a public setting. The local government is entitled to forgo or abandon the discussion altogether. If the agenda includes a reference to a planned executive session, upon the failure of the motion, it would be in order for the Presiding Officer to move to the next agenda item. See Rules 1.2 and 3.4.

Additionally, the rejection of a Motion for Executive Session is not a decision by the Body to waive any right to privilege or confidentiality that protects the information associated with the proposed session. As a rule, a waiver of privilege requires a *knowing* waiver by the Body,[140] and, because the Body is unaware of the specific information to be presented in the executive session, the Body lacks the requisite knowledge for an effective waiver.

CHAPTER 8

APPOINTMENT & ELECTION PROCESSES

From time to time, the appointment or election of either a Member of the Body or another person to a position of service to the local government is necessary or desired. This chapter offers procedures to aid the Body when making appointments or conducting elections in a fair, consistent, and effective manner.

23.0 Simple Appointment

Many appointments of Members or others to serve on committees, subcommittees, or in other positions of service to the Body or the government are not complicated. These uncomplicated appointments do not necessitate a formal process. For example, the Body may seek to appoint one of its Members or another person to serve on the local open space and trails committee or to act as the government's liaison with the local school district. When only one person seeks the appointment and there exists a consensus that the appointment is acceptable to the Body, a formal selection process is unwarranted.

The Body is authorized by the *Rules of Order* to forgo a formal nomination and election process when the Presiding Officer decides that there exists no competition or disagreement for an appointment. Simple appointment by a motion or an informal action will advance efficiency.

24.0 Formal Nomination & Election – Single Position

Local governments often find it necessary to formally elect a Member or another person to serve in a specific role within the Body or to serve on a board, commission, committee, subcommittee, or in another capacity. A formal process will advance fairness, especially where two or more persons seek the position. As examples, a municipal governing body may need to elect one of its Members to serve as the mayor, president, or mayor pro tem. A Body may also need to elect a Member to serve on a committee or subcommittee of the Body. A board of county commissioners may need to appoint the board chairperson or vice chairperson. A planning commission may need to elect from among its membership a person to serve as the chairperson or vice chairperson. A citizen may seek the Body's appointment to serve on a formally constituted board or commission.

Where two or more persons seek an available position, simple appointment pursuant to Section 23.0 is unavailable, and a formal election of a person to serve in that position may be necessary. Instead, Section 24.0 provides for a process for formal election in the event that two or more persons seek to fill a single available position.

Election Process

A. Generally

The following procedure shall apply to the Body's election of a person to serve in a special capacity on the Body or in a position on another body.

The process for the election shall be conducted during a regular or special meeting of the Body at which a quorum exists unless the bylaws or other governing policy of the Body provide for another process or procedure.

B. Determination of Process

1. Regular Process. The nomination and election process of Section 24.0 shall be followed unless the Body approves an alternative process.

2. Alternative Process. The Presiding Officer or another Member may offer a Principal Motion to the Body proposing the use of a process other than the process provided by Section 24.0. In order for the Principal Motion to be stated in clear and understandable language as required by Rule 5.2, the Moving Member shall provide to the Body in advance of the meeting a written process detailing the steps to be followed for the proposed alternative election process. The offered Principal Motion shall require a second and is debatable. See Section 15.0, Principal Motion.

The Body may, by a majority vote of a quorum on the Principal Motion (as it may be amended), require the use of the proposed alternative process. In such an event, the process for nominations and election provided by Section 24.0 will be modified as needed to comply with the Body-approved alternative election process.

C. **Nominations**

1. Nomination Required. To be eligible, a person seeking to fill a position must be nominated by a Member. If the position is available to be filled by a Member, a Member may nominate themselves.

2. Written Nominations. Nominations may be submitted in writing (which includes electronic mail and text messaging) to the Presiding Officer prior to the meeting at which nominations will be offered and accepted.

3. Nominations from the Floor. At the meeting, the Presiding Officer shall announce a call for nominations from the Floor.

4. Closing and Announcement. Upon a determination by the Presiding Officer that no further nominations are offered, the Presiding Officer shall announce that the opportunity for

nominations is closed. The Presiding Officer shall announce the name of each person who was nominated from the Floor and the name of any person for whom a written nomination was received prior to the meeting.

5. Acceptance of Nomination.

(a) For Positions of Leadership

Where the position to be filled is one of leadership[141] on the Body, the Presiding Officer shall obtain an acceptance of the nomination from each nominee to avoid the election of a Member unwilling to serve. Members expecting to be nominated but who will be absent from the meeting at which nominations will be offered must inform the Presiding Officer prior to the meeting of their willingness to accept a nomination for leadership in the event they are nominated. A Member who does not affirmatively express an acceptance of a nomination for leadership shall be deemed unwilling to serve if nominated and shall be excluded from candidacy in the election.

(b) For All Other Positions

To avoid election of a person unwilling to serve, the acceptance of a nomination is desired. The Presiding Officer shall endeavor to obtain an acceptance of the nomination by each person nominated. When the nominee is present, a simple verbal inquiry and confirmation of acceptance is sufficient. For absent nominees, acceptance may be expressed by a confirmation from the nominating Member that the nominee agreed to serve if elected, or written acceptance of a nomination from the nominee may be accepted. The Presiding Officer is authorized to forgo a need for a formal acceptance of a nomination where there is an understanding or expectation by the Body that the nominee will serve if elected.

6. Nomination of Presiding Officer. In the event that the Presiding Officer is nominated and accepts the nomination, the Presiding Officer shall temporarily relinquish the position as Presiding Officer to another Member in accordance with the Body's bylaws or other established policy.

D. Election

1. Selection of a Single Nominee. Should only one person be nominated for the available position, the Presiding Officer shall declare without vote that the nominated person is elected. The Presiding Officer's declaration is subject to a Point of Appeal. All Members of the Body, including any nominated Member, may vote on the Point of Appeal. Upon successful appeal by a majority of the Body, the appeal will require that a vote be conducted in order to elect the nominee.

2. Election from Multiple Nominees. In the event that two or more persons are nominated for one available position, an election from among the nominees shall be conducted.

3. Option for Nominee Statements. Prior to the casting of votes, the Presiding Officer may offer an opportunity to each nominee to provide a brief statement as to the nominee's qualifications for and interest in the position. In the interest of efficiency, the Presiding Officer may forgo the opportunity for statements or may set a uniform limit on

the duration of each nominee's statement. Nominees absent from the meeting may prepare a statement in advance and may request that a person in attendance read the nominee's statement if an opportunity for statements is offered and provided that the statement can be read within any time limitations set by the Presiding Officer.

4.   Process for Election. The Presiding Officer shall call for each Member's vote for a nominee.

(a)   For a leadership[142] position of the Body, the Presiding Officer may direct that the votes be cast by written secret ballot.[143] The Presiding Officer's direction is subject to a Point of Appeal. A Member who is a nominee may vote.

(b)   For all other positions, election shall be by any method acceptable to the Body that will allow the identity of the Member and the vote cast by each Member to be publicly known.[144] A Member who is a nominee may vote.

5.   Counting of Votes. The Presiding Officer or an administrative staff person shall be responsible for counting and publicly announcing the results of all voting. The Presiding Officer may appoint an administrative staff person to assist in verifying the accuracy of the vote. A vote cast for any person other than a nominee shall be invalid and not counted.

6.   Election Outcome. Based on the number of nominees and the resulting vote, the following determination and process shall be applied:

(a)   Election Between Two (2) Nominees – The nominee receiving the greater number of votes shall be declared elected. In the event of a tie vote between the two nominees, the Presiding Officer or administrative staff person shall conduct a drawing from among the names of the two nominees. The drawn nominee shall be declared elected.

(b) Between Three (3) or More Nominees – Should only one nominee receive the highest number of votes, the nominee shall be declared elected.

In the event that two or more nominees receive both the highest and the same number of votes (a tie vote), a revote shall be conducted from among the tied nominees only. Should only one nominee receive the highest number of votes, the nominee shall be declared elected. If upon revoting two or more nominees remain tied for the highest number of votes, the Presiding Officer or administrative staff person shall conduct a drawing from the names of the tied nominees, and the drawn nominee shall be declared elected.

25.0 Formal Nomination & Election - Multiple Positions

Local governments often encounter the need to fill multiple positions at one time on a single board, committee, subcommittee, or other Body. Multiple positions may arise, for example, with the initial creation of a committee or subcommittee or the need to fill positions created by the resignation of two Members of an existing committee. Individually filling each open position one at a time through the formal nomination and election process of Section 24.0 may be less efficient than filling the positions at one time from among a slate of nominees.

This section provides a process to fill multiple positions at one time.

Election Process

A. Generally

The following procedure shall apply for the election of two or more persons to fill two or more available positions on the Body, a committee, or subcommittee or to serve in appointed or representative positions on another Body.

The process for the election of persons shall be conducted during a regular or special meeting of the Body at which a quorum exists unless the bylaws or other governing policy of the Body provide for another process or procedure.

B. Determination of Process

1. Presiding Officer's Direction. Where multiple positions on a Body are to be filled at the same time, the Presiding Officer is authorized to direct the Body to follow the nomination and election process of Section 24.0[145] (filling each position individually) or Section 25.0 (filling multiple positions concurrently).

2. Alternative Process. A Member may offer a Principal Motion to the Body proposing the use of a process other than the process directed by the Presiding Officer. In order for the motion to be stated in clear and understandable language as required by Rule 5.2, the Moving Member shall provide to the Body in advance of the meeting a written process detailing the steps to be followed for the alternative selection process. The Principal Motion shall require a second and is debatable. See Section 15.0, Principal Motion.

   The Body may, by majority vote on the Principal Motion (as it may be amended), require the use of the proposed alternative process. In such an event, the process for nominations and selection or election provided by Section 25.0 will be modified as needed to comply with the Body-approved alternative selection process.

C. Nominations and Acceptance

Nominations and the acceptance of nominations shall follow the process provided by Section 24.0(C)(1) through (6) unless an alternative nomination process is approved by the Body.

D. Election

1. Nominees for Less than or Equaling the Number of Positions. Where the number of nominees is less than or equal to the number of available positions, the Presiding Officer shall declare without vote that the nominated members are all elected for the available positions. The Presiding Officer's declaration is subject to a Point of Appeal. All Members of the Body, including any nominees who are also Members, shall vote on any Point of Appeal. If a majority of a quorum voting on the appeal rejects the Presiding Officer's declaration, the election to the positions shall be addressed by filling each position individually in accordance with Section 24.0.

2. Election from Among More Nominees than Positions. If there are more nominations than available positions, an election from among all nominees shall be held. The Presiding Officer shall call, or shall direct an administrative staff person to call, for each Member's vote for nominees.

    When voting, each voting Member shall cast a vote by a written ballot identifying those nominees the Member desires to fill the number of open positions. The written ballot must include:

(a) at the top of the written ballot, the name of the Member casting the vote on the ballot; and

(b) the names of the persons the Member seeks to elect to available positions.

A Member who is also a nominee may vote and may vote for themselves. A Member need not cast a vote for a number of persons equal to the available number of positions. However, a ballot failing to identify the name of the Member voting or a ballot identifying a person other than a nominee or identifying a greater number of persons to be elected than available positions shall be declared invalid, and the vote of such a ballot shall not be counted.

3. Counting of Votes. The Presiding Officer or an administrative staff person shall be responsible for counting the votes on each ballot and publicly announcing the results of all voting. The Presiding Officer may appoint an administrative staff person to assist in verifying the accuracy of the vote.

All ballots shall be available for inspection by each Member of the Body and shall be a public record subject to inspection upon request.

4. Election Outcome. Based on the number of nominees, the number of available positions to be filled, and the resulting vote, the following process and determination shall apply:

(a) Where the votes cast identify that the number of available positions can be filled by the persons receiving the highest number of votes, then the Presiding Officer or administrative staff person shall announce the names of the persons elected to the available positions. For example:

Three (3) available positions are to be filled from among six (6) nominees. The voting outcome is:

Jones	6	**Elected**
Garcia	5	**Elected**
Smith	5	**Elected**
Johnson	4	Not Elected
Williams	1	Not Elected
Brown	0	Not Elected

(b) Where the votes cast identify that one or more of the available positions can be filled by one or more of the persons receiving the highest number of votes but a tie vote prevents a determination that all positions can be filled, the Presiding Officer or administrative staff person shall announce the names of the persons receiving the highest number of votes, who shall each be declared elected to an available position. A revote shall then be conducted from among all other remaining nominees for the position(s) that remain unfilled. Such a revoting process shall continue until a determination can be made that all available positions can be filled by persons receiving the highest number of votes. For example:

Three (3) available positions are to be filled from among six (6) nominees. The voting outcome is:

Jones	6	**Elected**
Garcia	5	**Elected**
Smith	4	Revote
Johnson	4	Revote
Williams	2	Revote
Brown	0	Revote

If the revote identifies that the remaining available positions can be filled with a nominee or nominees receiving the highest number of votes, the nominee or nominees receiving the highest number of votes shall be declared elected to the remaining positions. For example:

Following the election of Jones and Garcia above, one (1) available position remains. A revote from among the four (4) remaining nominees is held and results in election to the remaining position:

Smith	5	**Elected**
Johnson	3	Not Elected
Williams	2	Not Elected
Brown	0	Not Elected

If revoting fails to result in the election of the needed number of nominees for the available positions due to tie votes, the Presiding Officer may continue with a new revote from among the remaining nominees, proceed to a revote from among those nominees who each received the highest but same number of votes, or conduct a drawing from the names of the tied nominees, with the drawn nominee(s) being declared elected.

ADDITIONAL INFORMATION

Expert Advisors

I extend my sincere appreciation to the following exceptional people who assisted in the perspective, review, and editing of *Bob's Rules of Order*. They are each widely respected as recognized experts in local government law. I owe a debt to each of them, not only for their assistance with these *Rules of Order* but also for their long-standing support of Colorado local government.

David Broadwell

David Broadwell served Colorado municipalities for over 40 years, starting as a planner in Glenwood Springs in 1982. He was appointed as Glenwood's first full-time City Attorney from 1984 until 1992, when he moved to the Arvada City Attorney's office. He was a Colorado Municipal League (CML) staff attorney from 1992 to 1999 before joining the City and County of Denver as chief legal advisor to the Denver City Council. He is the principal author of *TABOR: A Guide to the Taxpayer's Bill of Rights* (1999) and contributed to numerous other CML publications while at CML. During his career, Mr. Broadwell was a frequent speaker on topics of interest to local government attorneys and officials, and between 1993 and 2015 he authored the chapter on local government law for the *Annual Survey of Colorado Law*, published by Continuing Legal Education in Colorado, Inc. In 2002, Mr. Broadwell received the Award for Distinguished Public Service by a Local Government Attorney from the International Municipal Law Association, and, in 2020, IMLA honored Mr. Broadwell with the Burk E. Delventhal Legal Advocacy Award. He re-joined the CML as General Counsel in 2019, where he served until his retirement in 2022.

Gerald Dahl

Gerald (Jerry) Dahl is a member of the Lakewood law firm of Murray Dahl Beery & Renaud LLP. Mr. Dahl serves as Town Attorney for Georgetown and Poncha Springs and City Attorney for Wheat Ridge, Colorado. A former General Counsel to the Northwest Colorado Council of Governments and the Colorado Municipal League, Mr. Dahl maintains a statewide practice in local government law, with particular expertise in annexation, land use, and elected official procedures. Mr. Dahl has mentored and supported innumerable Colorado local government attorneys throughout his career. Mr. Dahl can be reached at gdahl@mdbrlaw.com.

Sam Light

Sam Light is General Counsel for the Colorado Intergovernmental Risk Sharing Agency (CIRSA), a public entity self-insurance pool that provides property, liability, and workers' compensation insurance for Colorado cities, towns, and affiliated public entities. Prior to joining CIRSA in 2018, Mr. Light served in private practice with the Denver firm of Light Kelly P.C., where he practiced for over 20 years in the areas of municipal and public entity law and government liability and insurance issues. He served as General and Special Counsel to home rule and statutory municipalities and other public entities throughout Colorado and is a past president of the Colorado Municipal League Municipal Attorneys Section and the Metro City Attorneys Association. Mr. Light frequently provides training for local government elected and appointed officials and staff and frequently speaks at conferences on public entity risk management and related topics. He is the author of numerous articles, papers, and presentations on legal and risk-management issues affecting public entities, and he is a co-author and editor of CIRSA's *Ethics, Liability and Best Practices Handbook for Elected Officials*, which was awarded a national 2020 Outstanding Achievement Award by the Public Risk Management Association. Mr. Light can be reached at saml@cirsa. org.

Wynetta Massey

A native of Independence, Missouri, Wynetta Massey holds bachelor's degrees from the University of Missouri-Columbia in speech communication (with honors) and political science and graduated from the University of Kansas School of Law. She accepted a position with the Colorado Springs City Attorney's Office in 1990 and has served as Colorado Springs' City Attorney and Chief Legal Officer since 2014. Ms. Massey is a national speaker on a variety of municipal law topics, including ethics, land use, marijuana regulation, and the Council-Mayor form of government, and has published articles in *The Municipal Lawyer* and *The Kansas Municipal Law Annual*. She advances the practice of municipal law through the Colorado Municipal League (CML) and the International Municipal Lawyers Association (IMLA), serving on the executive boards of both organizations. Ms. Massey has chaired CML's Budget, Audit, and Management Committee, the *Amicus* Committee, and the Attorney's Section. She is a recipient of the IMLA *Amicus* Service Award and the James H. Epps Longevity in Service to a Community Award. Ms. Massey is also an IMLA Local Government Fellow and a nationally recognized expert in local government law. Ms. Massey may be reached at Wynetta.massey@ coloradosprings.gov.

Robert Sheesley

Robert Sheesley serves as General Counsel to the Colorado Municipal League (CML), where he supports and advises CML's municipal and associate members on the ever-changing laws affecting local government interests. Mr. Sheesley previously served as the City

Attorney for Commerce City, Colorado, and in the City Attorney's Office for the City of New Orleans. Before practicing municipal law, Mr. Sheesley practiced in the areas of commercial litigation and employment law in New Orleans and Jacksonville, Florida. A graduate of Loyola University New Orleans, Mr. Sheesley received his J.D. from the University of Florida College of Law and his M.P.A. from the University of Colorado Denver. Mr. Sheesley can be reached at rsheesley@cml.org.

ACKNOWLEDGEMENTS

An untold number of people played important roles during the last three decades in what is now *Bob's Rules of Order*. These people include mayors, governing body members, city and town managers and clerks, and seminar and conference attendees posing intriguing questions about parliamentary procedure.

Most notable among the local governments that assisted in *Bob's Rules* is the City of Centennial, Colorado. Incorporated in 2001 as one of Colorado's largest municipalities, Centennial strives to innovate and to create efficient processes and procedures in delivering services to its citizens. *Bob's Rules* is in large part premised on the meeting practices supported by Mayors Randy Pye, Cathy Noon, and Stephanie Piko and the truly exceptional city council members, city managers, and administrative staff that successfully led Centennial for more than 20 years. I owe to the City of Centennial my sincere and deepest appreciation.

My gratitude extends to the local government attorneys of Widner Juran LLP. Maureen Juran, Jill Hassman, Chris Price, Jennifer Madsen, and Molly Schultz each ably aided in the preparation of *Bob's Rules* with their exceptional insight, research, editing, and answers to my never-ending stream of questions about local government meeting procedures. You will not find a more experienced group of attorneys who are more devoted to the interests of Colorado local government. And I am proud to say that they are loyal friends.

The Colorado Municipal League (CML) also contributed to *Bob's Rules of Order*. During my entire career under the leadership of Kevin Bommer, Sam Mamet, and Ken Bueche, CML provided me with invaluable knowledge about local government and allowed me a forum to share my knowledge on local government topics and to present my ideas concerning effective public meetings.

Finally, and most deservingly, I extend my appreciation to my wife, Betsy, for her unwavering support of my passion and commitment to local government. Without her encouragement, *Bob's Rules of Order* would remain merely a pile of notes I collected throughout my career.

Notwithstanding everyone's exceptionally helpful aid and input, any error or deficiency in *Bob's Rules of Order* shall remain entirely my responsibility.

Bob Widner

ABOUT THE AUTHOR

Robert (Bob) Widner dedicated more than three decades to the representation of local governments through service as the city attorney, town attorney, county attorney, or special counsel for communities throughout Colorado. Bob's dedication to local government interests is demonstrated by his longstanding membership through statewide election to the Executive Board of the Colorado Municipal League (CML) and his election to lead CML as Board President.

Bob is the 2020 recipient of the Marvin J. Glink Private Practice Local Government Attorney Award conferred by the International Municipal Lawyers Association (IMLA). IMLA confers the award upon one attorney who best exemplifies excellence in the practice of municipal law and outstanding service to the public, has an exemplary reputation in the legal community, and exhibits a devotion to mentoring and educating young lawyers in local government law. Bob is one of fewer than 150 attorneys to receive an IMLA Fellowship as a recognized municipal law expert. As an adjunct professor of law with the University of Colorado Law School, Bob imparted his passion for local government and land-use law to students who now serve communities throughout the United States.

After fifteen years as an associate and a partner with the Denver law firm of Gorsuch Kirgis LLP, Bob founded the law firm of Widner Juran LLP in 2004. Widner Juran LLP exclusively represents the interests of Colorado local governments. Today, Bob continues his service as general and special counsel to Widner Juran's local government clients. Since 2004, Bob has served as the City Attorney for the City of Centennial, one of Colorado's larger municipalities and a nationally recognized leader in local government efficiency, effectiveness, and innovation. Bob is a frequent conference speaker and author of numerous publications and articles advancing the interests of local government.

Bob can be contacted at:

Robert Widner
Widner Juran LLP
13133 East Arapahoe Road, Suite 100
Centennial, Colorado 80112
rwidner@lawwj.com
www.lawwj.com

APPENDICES

Appendix A

Sample Form of Resolution for Adoption of *Bob's Rules of Order*

RESOLUTION NO. *XXX*

A RESOLUTION ADOPTING RULES OF ORDER FOR THE [*Name of Body*]

WHEREAS, the City of Somewhere is authorized to adopt procedures to govern the conduct of meetings and rules governing the decision-making process.

NOW, THEREFORE, BE IT RESOLVED BY THE CITY OF SOMEWHERE, COLORADO, AS FOLLOWS:

Section 1. The [*Name of Body authorized to adopt rules*] for the City of Somewhere hereby adopts as the rules of order governing meetings of the [*Name of Body*] the publication *Bob's Rules of Order for Colorado Local Governments* (Robert Widner, 2023 edition), with the following deletions or modifications:

Rule ____ is deleted in its entirety; and

Rule ____ is amended to provide that [*identify the rule change*].

Section 2. Effective Date. This Resolution shall take effect upon its approval by the [*Name of Body authorized to adopt rules*].

ADOPTED by a vote of ____ in favor and ____ against this ____ day of _____, 20__.

[*INSERT APPROVING BODY'S SIGNATURE BLOCK*]

APPENDIX B

Bob's Rules of Order

List of Rules for Reference

1.0   **The Meeting Generally**

Rule 1.1   Any state or local law that concerns the conduct of a meeting is a part of the *Rules of Order* to the extent the law is applicable to the Body.

Rule 1.2   The meeting agenda will be followed unless properly amended or modified.

Rule 1.3   The Body may presume that any legally required public notice for the meeting and for each agenda item was properly completed.

Rule 1.4   A Member shall disclose a conflict of interest and recuse themselves from both participation and voting when required by applicable state or local law.

Rule 1.5   A motion is not required for the Body to initiate discussion.

Rule 1.6   The record for each decision of the Body includes all information presented to the Body that pertains to the decision, all discussion and debate of the Body in reaching the decision, and all laws and local policies applicable to the decision.

Rule 1.7   The Body's decision on a matter is presumed to be supported by the record and by reasonable inferences drawn from the record.

Rule 1.8   A meeting formally ends only upon the Presiding Officer's declaration of adjournment without objection or upon the approval of a Motion to Adjourn.

2.0   The Quorum

Rule 2.1   A quorum of the Body is required for the Body to conduct business unless otherwise expressly provided by the Body's bylaws or the *Rules of Order*.

Rule 2.2   Unless otherwise provided by the Body's bylaws or other applicable law, a majority of the total membership of the Body who are present and eligible to vote shall constitute a quorum.

Rule 2.3   A request to be excused from the meeting while a motion is on the Floor, if granted, shall be effective:

+ Upon the granting of the request if the excuse is due to a lawfully recognized conflict of interest; or

+ Upon the granting of the request if the excused Member's absence will not deny the Body of a quorum; or

+ Upon the final vote or other final resolution of the pending motion if the excused Member's absence will deny the Body of a quorum.

Rule 2.4   A Member's unexcused absence while a motion is on the Floor shall not affect the quorum until the final vote or other final resolution of the motion.

Rule 2.5   In the absence of a quorum, the Presiding Officer, the Members present, or an administrative staff member shall:

✦ Postpone all unresolved agenda items to the next regular meeting; and

✦ Adjourn the meeting.

3.0 The Presiding Officer

Rule 3.1   The Presiding Officer shall be the exclusive director and facilitator of all meeting conduct.

Rule 3.2   The Presiding Officer serves as the parliamentarian unless the role is assigned to another person.

Rule 3.3   The Presiding Officer is entitled to the same rights as a Member unless otherwise limited by law.

Rule 3.4   The Presiding Officer may exercise discretion during the meeting subject to a Point of Order or a Point of Appeal.

Rule 3.5   The Presiding Officer shall facilitate the meeting in a fair and neutral manner and, whenever practicable, defer to the Members to initially lead discussion, offer motions, and direct debate.

4.0 The Floor

Rule 4.1   The Floor is required to address the Body.

Rule 4.2   A Member shall be granted the Floor by the Presiding Officer when properly requested in accordance with the *Rules* and local meeting practice.

Rule 4.3   A Member's right to the Floor is limited to five minutes.

Rule 4.4   A Member may obtain the Floor only once until all other Members are afforded an opportunity to obtain the Floor.

5.0   The Motion & Second

Rule 5.1   A motion is required for the Body to take formal action.

Rule 5.2   A motion shall propose an affirmative proposition in clear and understandable language that is limited to either a "yes" or a "no" vote.

Rule 5.3   A motion requires a second.

Rule 5.4   To be placed on the Floor for the Body's consideration, the Presiding Officer must acknowledge that the motion was properly stated and seconded in accordance with Rules 5.2 and 5.3.

Rule 5.5   A motion, once acknowledged by the Presiding Officer and placed on the Floor, is owned by the Body.

Rule 5.6   The Presiding Officer shall offer the Moving Member the first opportunity to speak to a debatable motion.

6.0   The Friendly Requests

Rule 6.1   A Friendly Amendment is authorized only for a debatable motion, and the amendment of the motion will be effective unless a Member objects.

Rule 6.2   A Friendly Withdrawal is authorized only for a debatable motion, and the withdrawal of the motion will be effective unless a Member objects.

7.0   The Vote

Rule 7.1   The Presiding Officer's call for the vote closes the Floor.

Rule 7.2   Proxy or absentee voting is not permitted.

Rule 7.3   A Member's attempt to explain their vote after the call for the vote is not permitted.

Rule 7.4   Neither the Moving Member nor the Member offering a second on a motion must advocate for or vote in favor of the motion.

Rule 7.5   Each Member eligible to vote on a motion shall vote either "yes" or "no."

Rule 7.6   The approval of a motion requires a vote of a majority of a quorum unless a greater number of votes is required by the *Rules of Order* or by law.

Rule 7.7   The approval of a motion by the required vote shall decisively approve the motion's proposition or question.

Rule 7.8   The failure of a motion to receive the required vote for approval shall result in the rejection of the motion.

Rule 7.9   A Member shall not change their vote after the announcement of the final vote except in exceptional circumstances with the approval of the Presiding Officer.

8.0   Rule Suspension and Rule Deviation

Rule 8.1   The Presiding Officer may suspend certain rules.

Rule 8.2   The Body may suspend certain rules.

Rule 8.3   An inadvertent and non-substantive deviation from a rule by the Presiding Officer or the Body without objection from a Member is authorized and intended.

10.0   Points Generally

Rule 10.1   A point is privileged and may be raised at any time.

Rule 10.2   A point does not require the Floor.

Rule 10.3   A point does not require a second.

14.0   **Motions Generally**

Rule 14.1   A main motion is only in order when no other motion is on the Floor.

Rule 14.2   A debatable motion may be amended by either:

+ A Friendly Amendment pursuant to Rule 6.1; or

+ A Motion to Amend.

Rule 14.3   Only one Motion to Amend may be on the Floor at any one time.

APPENDIX C

Bob's Rules of Order

<u>Summary Table of Points and Motions</u>

TYPE	MOTION	FLOOR?	WHEN IN ORDER?	SECOND?	DEBAT-ABLE?	VOTE?
POINT	Order	No	Any time	No	No	No
	Information	No	Any time	No	No	No
	Appeal	No	Immediately following Presiding Officer's decision	No	No	Majority of quorum
MAIN	Principal Motion	Yes	When no motion is pending	Yes	Yes	Majority of quorum usually but may depend on special law. Rule 7.6
	Reconsider	Yes	When no motion is pending but with limited availability. Section 19	Yes	Yes, only as to the reason to recon-sider	2/3 of quorum
	Adjourn	Yes	When no motion is pending	Yes	Yes	Majority of quorum

TYPE	MOTION	FLOOR?	WHEN IN ORDER?	SECOND?	DEBAT-ABLE?	VOTE?
MAIN	**Continue or Postpone**	Yes	When no motion is pending	Yes	Yes	Majority of quorum
		Yes	When a Principal Motion is pending	Yes	Yes	Majority of quorum
SUBSIDIARY	**Amend** a pending debat-able motion	Yes	When a debatable motion is pending	Yes	Yes	Majority of quorum
	Close Debate	Yes	When a debatable motion is pending	Yes	No	2/3 of quorum
PRIVILEGED	**Recess**	Yes	Any time	Yes	No	Majority of quorum
	Executive Session	Yes	Any time	Yes	No	2/3 of quorum

173

ENDNOTES

1   Sometimes also referred to as "parliamentary rules" or "rules of procedure."

2   The term "parliamentary" when associated with rules is generally used today to describe rules that govern the decision-making process of deliberative bodies. The word originates from early medieval English to identify a legislative Body assembled by the British sovereign comprised of nobility, clergy, and commoners.

3   Henry M. Robert III et al., *Robert's Rules of Order Newly Revised*, 12th ed. (New York: Public Affairs, 2020). Within the endnotes of *Bob's Rules of Order*, the 12th edition of *Robert's Rules of Order Newly Revised* is abbreviated as "*RONR*."

4   To its credit, the publishers of *RONR* recognize the length and complexity of the rules and offer a 213-page *Robert's Rules of Order in Brief* (referred to herein as *In Brief*). On the inside cover of *In Brief*, the publishers caution that the *In Brief* edition serves as an introduction and guide to *RONR* and is only a "partial summary" that is not suitable for use as a body's parliamentary authority. See Henry M. Robert III et al., *Robert's Rules of Order Newly Revised in Brief*, 3rd ed. (New York: Public Affairs, 2020).

5   *RONR* includes 41 pages of a table of contents, preface, and introduction; 633 pages of principal text; 52 pages of charts, tables, and lists; a 14-page appendix; and a 63-page index, totaling 803 pages.

6   See *RONR*, Table of Rules Relating to Motions, at pages t6–t33.

7   Allen C. Jennings, *Robert's Rules for Dummies*, 4th ed. (New Jersey: John Wiley & Sons Inc., 2022).

8   Nancy Sylvester, *The Complete Idiot's Guide to Robert's Rules,* 2nd ed. (New York: Penguin, 2010) (published prior to the 12th edition of *RONR*).

9   Not surprisingly given the 803 pages and complexity of *RONR*, individuals seeking to gain a minimum or an advanced level of competence in *RONR* may pursue professional registration or certification. The National Association of Parliamentarians (NAP) offers credentialing processes that include testing of the individual's proficiency in the use of *RONR*. See https://www.parliamentarians.org. The American Institute of Parliamentarians (AIP) applies the *Standard Code of Parliamentary Procedure* (citation at footnote 14) in its credentialing processes, which also includes a testing process to achieve certification. See https://www.aipparl.org. Without doubt, requiring all members of a local governmental body to study, test, and gain a certified level of competency in the use of either *RONR* or the *Standard Code of Parliamentary Procedure* will aid the members in using these complex sets of meeting rules. Such a commitment of time, effort, and funding to learn rules more complex than needed for local government meetings may, however, be unwarranted for most governments.

10   Ann G. Macfarlane and Andrew L. Estep's *Mastering Council Meetings* (Seattle, ERGA, Inc. 2013) published by Jurassic Parliament offers a "guidebook for elected officials and local governments." The guidebook is not a complete set of rules of order. Instead, the guidebook seeks to assist readers in applying *RONR* to government meetings and conducting meetings "according to Robert." Because it is entirely based on *RONR*, the guidebook retains the deficiencies of *RONR* when applied to local government meetings and recognizes that quasi-judicial hearings are "outside the scope of the book." Although *Mastering*

Council Meetings is an entertaining stroll through *RONR*, the book cannot serve as a set of rules of order for local government bodies. *Mastering Council Meetings* is, however, recommended for its practical and useful ideas on the management of a public meeting.

11   The number of instances that *RONR* will conflict with the common needs of local government meetings are too many to summarize. Examples can be found in Chapter XX concerning Disciplinary Procedures, which authorizes the imposition of penalties against members who do not follow the provisions of *RONR*, including a censure or suspension or mandating an apology from a member and the exclusion of a member from a meeting until the member offers the apology. *RONR* § 61:15, page 611. *RONR* also authorizes the body to remove the mayor, chairperson, or other presiding officer as the director of the meeting. See Interpretive Rule 2006-02 at https://robertsrules. com/official-interpretations/#interpretations.

12   The formality imposed on meetings by *RONR* contributes to the sheer size of the volume of rules and the rules' complexity. As a few examples found at *RONR* §§ 3:10–3:13, pages 20–22, *RONR* limits the words that members may use when referring to the presiding officer and the other members of leadership, prohibits the use of the word "you" when referring to the presiding officer or other members except in limited circumstances, requires the presiding officer to refer to themselves in the third person, and prohibits members from using the names of other members. These, and other formal meeting mandates, make much of *RONR* inconsistent with the more casual or collaborative character of the typical local government meeting. *RONR* recognizes that a "small board" can abide by a few different and less formal rules than a larger body, such as allowing the presiding officer and

members to remain seated when addressing the body. However, *RONR* buries a few references to special rules for small boards throughout its text in random clauses and sentences, and some exceptions to the mandates of *RONR* can be found in a single one-half page section among the 803 total pages in Chapter XVI, § 49:21. With the very few exceptions for small boards, all other rules of *RONR* apply to a meeting of a small board.

13 By way of only one example, *RONR* authorizes the presiding officer to unilaterally expel any nonmember (i.e., a citizen) from a meeting because nonmembers hold no right to attend a meeting. *RONR* § 61:7, page 609. This and other provisions of *RONR* conflict with Colorado's statutory requirements for local governments, including the Colorado Open Meeting Law.

14 As examples, see the American Institute of Parliamentarians, *Standard Code of Parliamentary Procedure* (New York: McGraw Hill, 2012); and O. Garfield Jones, *Parliamentary Procedure at a Glance* (New York: Penguin, 1971). At 326 pages in length, the *Standard Code* includes motions and procedures not commonly used or needed during the typical local government meeting. *Parliamentary Procedure at a Glance* is based on *RONR* editions predating the current 12th edition.

15 See Hartley v. City of Colorado Springs, 764 P.2d 1216 (Colo. 1988) (governing body's adoption of meeting rules granted jurisdiction to conduct meetings in accordance with the rules); City of Greeley v. Hamman, 28 P. 460 (Colo. 1891) (where no constitutional or statutory obligation exists to require specific meeting procedure, a governing body is authorized to adopt rules to govern its proceedings); Glenwood Post v. City of Glenwood Springs, 731 P.2d 761 (Colo. App. 1986) (local government may adopt its own rules of order). See also E. McQuillin, *The Law of*

Municipal Corporations, §§ 13:66–13:67 (3ʳᵈ edition, 2019) (citing numerous state judicial decisions supporting the authority of governmental bodies to adopt rules of order and procedure to govern meetings).

16   *Bob's Rules of Order* does not authorize a Body to conduct virtual meetings. The authorization for the use of different forms of meetings should be addressed by the Body's bylaws or other local policy of the local government.

17   Very generally and in the context of local government meetings and hearings, the constitutional right of procedural due process requires the government to establish and follow processes and procedures designed to ensure fairness to individuals holding a protected property interest. Countless judicial decisions acknowledge that the existence of rules and the compliance with established rules leads to fairness in the administration of laws and government programs.

18   See, e.g., C.R.S. § 31-16-103 (municipal ordinances to be published and recorded in a book to be received as evidence) and C.R.S. §§ 30-11-101, 30-15-401, and 30-15-404 (county laws to be published and recorded). Assuredly, the written law formally adopted by federal, state, and local governments will govern the actions of these respective governments. In addition, unwritten rules, principals, and norms that are consistently followed can, at times, be referenced to support or guide the government's actions.

19   As some examples of courts finding that action taken in accordance with adopted procedural rules of order will be deemed authorized, see L.C. Canyon Partners v. Salt Lake County, 266 P.3d 797 (Utah 2011) (rules expressly authorized action to reconsider and to rescind a decision); Hartley v. City

of Colorado Springs, 764 P.2d 1216 Colo. 1988) (rules of order granted authority to reconsider a prior decision); McGuire v. City of Sweetwater, Tennessee, No. 20-6067, 2021 WL 3620449 (6th Cir. Aug. 16, 2021) (denying citizens the right to speak was authorized by adopted meeting rules of order); Wolfman, Inc. v. City of New Orleans, 874 So. 2d 261 (La. Ct. App. 2004) (board's failure to follow its procedural meeting rules invalidated a decision); Marohn's Buffalo Marketplace v. City of Buffalo, 2002 WL 31819273 (Minn. Ct. App. 2002) (a non-technical defect in following adopted procedural rules proved fatal to a zoning decision).

20   Consistent with *Bob's Rules*, *RONR* recognizes the difference between bylaws and rules of order and also recognizes the confusion that can result when combining or integrating rules of order with bylaws due to important differences in the subject matter and the ability to amend and suspend the rules of the two different documents. *RONR* also recognizes bylaws as being the most important organizational document for the body and that the bylaws will expressly recognize the parliamentary procedure to be applied by the body in the conduct of its meetings. See *RONR*, Chapter XVIII, pages 535–567, and Chapter I, pages 11–13. Similarly, the National Association of Parliamentarians (NAP) recognizes that bylaws and parliamentary procedures/rules of order are not the same. See https://www.parliamentarians.org/wp-content/uploads/2019/10/NAP-Bylaws-2019-Final.pdf.

21   Besides the title "bylaws," some bodies use other titles for the principal governing document for the body, such as "rules of procedure," "rules of procedure and order," "code of procedure," "code of conduct," "meeting regulations," or "meeting guidelines," and at times integrate what is commonly recognized as bylaws with decision-making rules of order into

a single document sometimes titled "rules of order." Both *Bob's Rules of Order* and *RONR* suggest not to combine the bylaws with procedural rules of order because these forms of regulations serve two different purposes.

22   Whether to authorize a Body to conduct video conference meetings (i.e., remote attendance via an online video conference platform such as Zoom, Microsoft Teams, Adobe Connect, GoToMeeting, and Facebook Messenger) is an issue that each local government should consider in its bylaws. Video conference meetings present practical implications and legal issues when conducting these types of nontraditional meetings, with implications and issues largely stemming from requirements of due process and fairness in the quasi-judicial setting.

23   See *RONR*, Chapter V, pages 92–115, The Main Motion.

24   As an example, *RONR* classifies more than 30 motions or motion variations as "main motions," but the phrase "main motion" is also used by *RONR* to describe the primary or principal business motion. See *RONR*, Chapter V, pages 92–115, and Table of Rules Relating to Motions, *RONR*, pages t6–t33.

25   Appendix A at the end of this handbook includes a sample form of a resolution for the adoption of *Bob's Rules*.

26   By way of an example of a potential rule modification, Rule 7.5 provides that voting on all motions should be a "yes" or "no" vote. A Member's vote to "abstain," a Member's silence, or another declaration other than "yes" or "no" is out of order. However, a Body may decide that, after reviewing the rationale of Rule 7.5 and consulting with the Body's legal counsel, abstentions should nonetheless be permitted. Another example of a desired modification may be to Rule 4.3, which limits a

Member's right to the Floor on any matter to a maximum of five minutes unless otherwise authorized by the Presiding Officer. The local government may feel that a time lesser or greater than five minutes, or no time limit at all, should be the recognized rule for the Body.

27   The practice of modifying or amending standardized, uniform, or model regulations and general codes is common. For example, most local governments modify or amend provisions of the International Building Code or the Model Traffic Code at the time of the adoption of these codes by ordinance. *Bob's Rules* uses a numbering system for each rule, point, and motion to enable adopting local governments to identify the provision subject to modification or amendment.

28   For a debriefing of a quasi-judicial decision, the Body's legal counsel may advise that the session be conducted after the expiration of any right of appeal for the decision. For decisions that involve significant or substantive errors, the legal counsel may advise that an executive session be held to receive legal advice regarding the meeting process and the proper application of the *Rules*.

29   See Cherry Hills Resort Development Co. v. City of Cherry Hills Village, 757 P.2d 622 (Colo. 1988).

30   The term "quasi-judicial" (rather than "judicial") is commonly used when referring to the exercise of judicial power by local government officials. The officials are not held to the strict requirements of judges in a court of law but serve in a role that is very similar to a judge. "Quasi" means "having some resemblance by having certain attributes." *Merriam-Webster Online Dictionary*, https://www.merriam-webster.com/dictionary/ quasi. For an excellent summary of the requirements for quasi-judicial action,

see the Colorado Intergovernmental Risk Sharing Agency's (CIRSA) Quasi-Judicial Basic Training presentation prepared by Sam Light, CIRSA General Counsel, at https://www.cirsa.org/wp-content/uploads/2020/05/Quasi-JudicialProceedings.pdf.

31   For an explanation and comparison of quasi-judicial action in the local government context, see Jafay v. Boulder County Comm'rs, 848 P.2d 892 (Colo. 1993); Prairie Dog Advocates v. City of Lakewood, 20 P.3d 1203 (Colo. 2000).

32   City of Aurora v. Zwerdlinger, 571 P.2d 1074 (Colo. 1977).

33   *Discussion*, Black's Law Dictionary, page 567 (10th ed. 2014).

34   See https://www.dictionary.com/browse/discussion

35   See https://www.dictionary.com/browse/debate

36   See https://www.merriam-webster.com/dictionary/debate

37   The term "postpone" means "to change the date or time for a planned event or action to a later one." In contrast, "continue" and more specifically the phrase "continued meeting" means "a meeting that is part of a session that will be … resumed after adjournment." See definitions of *Postpone*, *Continue*, and *Continued meeting*, Black's Law Dictionary, pages 1132 and 1356 (10th ed. 2014).

38   *Abstention*, Black's Law Dictionary, page 10 (10th ed. 2014).

39   *Recusal*, Black's Law Dictionary, page 1467 (10th ed. 2014).

40   Legal impediments to voting will commonly result from state statutory provisions concerning conflicts of interest. In addition, the local government's charter, ordinances, bylaws, or code of ethics may impose special requirements on voting that are binding on the Body and its Members. It is important that

Members consult with the local legal counsel regarding voting requirements.

41   Some rules of order, including *RONR*, provide for a separately recognized "motion to amend the agenda." *Bob's Rules* relies upon a Principal Motion as the means to formally amend the agenda for several reasons: (1) the agenda will not often need amending, and creating a separate motion adds unneeded clutter to the *Rules*; (2) a Presiding Officer's discretionary modification of an agenda pursuant to Rule 3.4 is rarely opposed because the modification is readily seen by the Body as acceptable and necessary for efficiency; and (3) the use of a Principal Motion to amend the agenda is no different than a motion to amend the agenda because both motions require the Moving Member to state the specific amendment and to obtain a majority vote from a quorum.

42   Many actions by local government require specialized notice apart from the general meeting notice. As some examples, a separate public notice in addition to the general notice for the public meeting is required for (1) a hearing to change the zone district of property or to adopt or change development regulations, (2) the legislative approval of the local government's budget, and (3) the annexation of property. See C.R.S. § 31-23-304 (zoning and development regulations); C.R.S. § 29-1-106 (budget hearing); and C.R.S. § 31-12-108 (annexation hearing).

43   See C.R.S. § 24-6-402(2)(c)(I).

44   A "meeting" is defined by the Colorado Open Meetings Law as "any kind of gathering convened to discuss public business, in person, by telephone, electronically, or by other means of communication." C.R.S. § 24-6-402 (1)(b).

45   C.R.S. § 24-6-402 (2)(c)(I).

46   As a widely accepted general rule, notice of public meetings and hearings requires information sufficient to reasonably apprise an interested person of the date, time, place, and general purpose of the meeting or hearing. See, e.g., Hallmark Builders v. City of Gunnison, 650 P.2d 556, 559 (Colo. 1982); Whatley v. Summit County Bd. of County Comm'rs., 77 P.3d 793, 801 (Colo. App. 2003). For meetings conducted after July 1, 2019, the Colorado Open Meetings Law directs that the local public body "post the notice, with specific agenda information if available, no less than 24 hours prior to the holding of the meeting on a public website of the local public body." C.R.S. § 24-6-402 (2)(c)(I). Local law or policy may require other forms of notice.

47   As an example of a requirement for the issuance of multiple notices for a hearing, see C.R.S. § 31-12-108 (municipal annexation of land).

48   See note 42.

49   See Standards of Conduct, Article 18 of Title 24, C.R.S. (*Code of Ethics* and *Proscribed Acts Related to Contracts and Claims*) and C.R.S. § 18-8-308 (*Failing to Disclose a Conflict of Interest*).

50   See Chapter 2, Special Terminology, "Abstain" and "Recuse."

51   *RONR* prohibits or discourages any discussion prior to a motion. For example, *RONR*, § 4:7 on page 30 states that, "under parliamentary procedure, strictly speaking, discussion of any subject is permitted only with reference to a pending motion." In addition, *RONR* states that "[t]he general rule against discussion without a motion is one of the parliamentary procedure's powerful tools for keeping business 'on track,' and an observance of its spirit can be an important factor in making even a

very small meeting rapidly moving and interesting." *RONR*, § 4:8, page 31. For a "small board," *RONR* allows for informal discussion without a motion, although what may be "informal" is undefined by *RONR*. *RONR*, § 49:21, pages 464–465. It may prove inefficient for the Body to expend time entertaining and deciding objections concerning whether a particular discussion is "informal" and demands by one or more Members that the Body cease discussion in order to comply with *RONR*.

52 See note 53. It could be viewed as unfair in a judicial proceeding for the judge to announce at the outset of the proceeding and prior to the presentation of any evidence that she is proposing to rule against one of the parties.

53 See, e.g., Wells v. Del Norte School Dist., 753 P.2d 770, 772 (Colo. App. 1987); Soon Yee Scott v. City of Englewood, 672 P.2d 225, 227 (Colo. App. 1983); Omar T. McMahon, *A Fair Trial Before Quasi-Judicial Tribunals as Required by Due Process*, 29 Marq. L. Rev. 95 (1948).

54 A Member sitting as a judge in a quasi-judicial proceeding may offer or acknowledge factual testimony in a very limited circumstance, called "judicial notice." The Member may express a fact that is not subject to reasonable dispute because it (a) is generally known (such as the sun rises in the east) or (b) can be accurately and readily determined from sources whose accuracy cannot reasonably be questioned. Judicial notice is a very limited and specialized exception that allows a judge to express or to accept a fact that "everyone already knows."

55 A quasi-judicial decision may be challenged in a state court pursuant to Rule 106(a)(4) of the Colorado Rules of Civil Procedure. According to Colorado courts and Rule 106(a)(4), a court may invalidate a Body's decision if there is no competent

evidence to support the decision. "No competent evidence" means that there is an absence of evidence in the record to support the ultimate decision of the Body, and the decision is found to be arbitrary and capricious. See, e.g., McCann v. Lettig, 928 P.2d 816 (Colo. App. 1996); Board of County Commissioners of Routt County v. O'Dell, 920 P.2d 48 (Colo. 1996); Carney v. Civil Service Commission, 30 P.3d 861 (Colo. App. 2001); Cruzen v. Career Services Board, 899 P.2d 373 (Colo. App. 1995).

56   Not all meetings of a Body must follow the same quorum requirement. For example, a Body's bylaws may provide that a workshop or study session where no formal decisions may be made can be conducted with a quorum different than the quorum necessary to conduct formal business and vote on motions binding the Body.

57   Legal counsel will most often advise that the Body must refrain from discussion of a quasi-judicial matter unless a quorum of the Body is present and proper notice of the meeting was issued.

58   A meeting pursuant to the Colorado Open Meetings Law (COML) is defined as "any kind of gathering, convened to discuss public business, in person, by telephone, electronically, or by other means of communication." C.R.S. § 24-6-402 (1)(b). COML recognizes that meetings "at which any public business is discussed … are declared to be public meetings open to the public at all times." C.R.S. § 24-6-402 (2)(b).

59   Rule 2.2 and the meaning of the phrase "total membership" in the context of a quorum is consistent with C.R.S. § 2-4-111 (defining as a matter of statutory construction that a "quorum of a public body is a majority of the number of members fixed by statute."). The meaning is also consistent with C.R.S. § 31-1-

101(4) (definition of "governing body" that provides that, "[f]or purposes of determining a quorum or the required number of votes for any matter, 'governing body' includes the total number of seats on the governing body but does not include the seat held by a nonvoting city manager under section 31-4-214."). Note that setting a quorum requirement based upon the total number of persons *attending* the meeting can lead to an unacceptable result. For example, if the quorum requirement for a meeting of a seven-member body is a majority of the "members present" or "in attendance" and only three members attend the meeting, a motion that requires a vote of a majority of the members present or in attendance may be approved with only two affirmative votes or far less than a majority of the total membership of the Body.

60   The Body's bylaws or other policy should describe what constitutes a presence at a meeting, which may include, in addition to actual physical presence, participation by telephone or attendance through a video conferencing platform such as Zoom, Microsoft Teams, Adobe Connect, GoToMeeting, or Facebook Messenger.

61   Many local government bodies recognize positions for one or more nonvoting members on the Body. These positions may be titled as an "ex officio," an "alternate," an "associate," or a "liaison" member. Although the persons in these positions may sit at the dais and may take part in discussion and debate, these members are not eligible to vote except, where provided by the bylaws or other policy, when the member is authorized to fill a voting position in the event of an absence of a voting Member. It is the total number of authorized voting positions on the Body (which is a number set by state or local law, the bylaws, or other governing policy) and not the total voting and nonvoting

positions that will comprise a quorum for purposes of the *Rules of Order*.

62   The Body's bylaws should describe the accepted justifications for an excused absence and who may grant the excuse. Many bylaws provide that the Presiding Officer is authorized to grant an excuse when justified and that the Presiding Officer's decision is subject to a Point of Appeal.

63   If the quorum was established with the minimum number of Members necessary for a quorum, the absence of an *excused* Member will deny the Body of a quorum and the ability to conduct business and make decisions. Such an impact on the quorum in such circumstances is an unfortunate aspect of a public meeting and the quorum requirement.

64   Most motions require a majority or a supermajority of a quorum. With each absence of a Member from the meeting, the number of votes needed for approval of a motion may be more difficult to achieve—that is, securing a majority vote of four Members from a seven-member Body when all seven Members are in attendance is more achievable than securing three votes from only four Members in attendance from the same seven-member Body. An emergency ordinance, as another example, requires three-fourths of the entire membership of the governing body. When only six Members are present and eligible to vote from a seven-member Body, a unanimous vote of all six Members will be necessary for approval of the emergency ordinance. When the quorum requirement is satisfied for a seven-member Body with fewer than six Members, the Body cannot enact an emergency ordinance. See C.R.S. § 31-16-105.

65　The Body's legal counsel should be consulted about any need to re-publish or re-post new hearing notices for a postponed quasi-judicial hearing.

66　Note that Rule 3.3 takes a different approach from the general requirements of *RONR*, which provide that the chairperson may not participate in discussion or debate unless the chairperson formally relinquishes the chair to another member of the body. *RONR*, Chapter XII, § 43:29, page 374. However, Rule 3.3 is consistent with the rules in *RONR* as applied to a "small board." For small boards, *RONR* allows the chairperson to speak in "informal discussion." *RONR*, Chapter XVI, § 49:21, pages 464–465. Unfortunately, *RONR* does not define what constitutes "informal discussion," and this deficiency can potentially lead to conflict when members believe that the chairperson's comments during discussion are not informal. Equally unhelpful in applying *RONR* in this case is the common definition of "informal," which generally means "marked by the absence of formality or ceremony." See *Merriam-Webster Online Dictionary* at https://www.merriam-webster.com/dictionary/informal

67　See C.R.S. § 31-4-302, which applies to a municipal board of trustees. This section provides that "an ordinance limiting the mayor's power may provide that the mayor shall not be counted for purposes of deciding a quorum or for the requisite majority on any matter to be voted on by the board of trustees."

68　Id.

69　Concurrence or consent is often expressed by an absence of any objection from the Members upon the Presiding Officer's proposal to take an action. Some Presiding Officers ask for a show of hands or pose an inquiry of "Thumbs up?" or "Any objections?" to solicit the Body's general consent in place of a formal vote.

70   When the Presiding Officer holds the office of mayor, the passing of the gavel to another Member does not relieve the mayor from any statutory, charter, or other limitation imposed on the office of mayor. For example, in a statutory town, an ordinance may be adopted to deny the mayor the right to vote except in the event of a tie vote. See C.R.S. § 31-4-302. Assigning the role of Presiding Officer to another Member will not relieve the mayor from this statutory limitation. The passing of the gavel only authorizes another Member to conduct the meeting in the role of Presiding Officer.

71   This informal concurrence or consent is often expressed by an absence of any objection from the Members upon the Presiding Officer's proposal to take an action. Some Presiding Officers ask for a show of hands or pose an inquiry of "Thumbs up?" or "Any objections?" to solicit the Body's general consent in place of a formal vote.

72   In some limited circumstances, the local home rule charter, ordinance, or policy may provide that the Body may only act by ordinance, resolution, or motion. This type of limitation could be interpreted to prohibit all use of an informal consensus by the Body, even for minor matters. The Body should consult with its legal counsel when deciding the proper interpretation of any charter, ordinance, or other policy provisions that may limit the authority to render decisions informally.

73   Although reference is made in *Bob's Rules* to the expression of "yes" or "no" regarding a Member's vote, other affirmative expressions such as "aye" or "nay" are not precluded by the

Rules if the expression clearly informs the Body of the Member's vote.

74　It would be unfair for the Moving Member to speak to a motion that is <u>not</u> debatable because the other Members would not share the same opportunity to comment or debate. A nondebatable motion asks the Body to take a defined and specific action, which does not require Members to engage in a detailed evaluation of viewpoints or to debate the possible impacts or effects of the motion.

75　A Friendly Amendment is premised on the practice of unanimous consent as recognized by *RONR*, Chapter II, §§4:59–4:62, pages 49–51.

76　The debatable motions are the Principal Motion, Motion to Continue or Postpone, Motion to Amend, Motion to Reconsider, and Motion to Adjourn.

77　A Member may also express the objection by a Point of Order to require the Body to comply with Rule 5.1 and to entertain the amendment by a formal Motion to Amend.

78　The debatable motions are the Principal Motion, Motion to Continue or Postpone, Motion to Amend, Motion to Reconsider, and Motion to Adjourn.

79　A Friendly Withdrawal is premised on the idea of unanimous consent found in several publications and also recognized by *RONR* in Chapter II, §§ 4:58–4:63, pages 49–51.

80　The Body's bylaws should address what constitutes attendance (or presence), which may include attendance by telephonic or virtual means in addition to physical presence. Most bylaws will effectively prohibit voting by proxy when the quorum determination is based upon physical presence in the meeting or upon authorized virtual or telephonic attendance.

81 Most often, the Member granting the proxy will not attend the meeting, although absence from the meeting is not typically a requirement to grant a proxy.

82 Procedural due process for a quasi-judicial matter requires that the persons deciding the matter enter the hearing as neutral and unbiased judges and render a decision based only on the evidence presented during the hearing. See, e.g., Wells v. Del Norte School Dist., 753 P.2d 770, 772 (Colo. App. 1987); Soon Yee Scott v. City of Englewood, 672 P.2d 225, 227 (Colo. App. 1983); Omar T. McMahon, *A Fair Trial Before Quasi-Judicial Tribunals as Required by Due Process*, 29 Marq. L. Rev. 95 (1948).

83 *RONR* and one set of uniform rules of order offered to local government officials prohibit a member making a motion from speaking against the member's own motion. *RONR*, § 43:25, pages 372–373; Ann G. Macfarlane and Andrew L. Estep, *Mastering Council Meetings* (Seattle, ERGA, Inc. 2013), at Appendix C, page 115.

84 Recall that the Moving Member is afforded the first right to the Floor to speak to the motion pursuant to Rule 5.6. In this initial address to the Body, Rules 5.6 and 7.4 allow the Moving Member the opportunity to explain that the motion is offered only to allow debate, and the Moving Member can offer reasons why the Body should reject the motion.

85 Although *Bob's Rules* references the expression of a "yes" or a "no" vote regarding a motion, other affirmative expressions such as "aye" or "nay" are not precluded by the *Rules* if the expression clearly informs the Body of the Member's vote.

86   See Chapter 2, Special Terminology, "Abstain" and "Recuse." See also Chapter 1, Incorporating *Bob's Rules* into Meeting Practice, for guidance on changing the *Rules* to recognize a right to abstain when voting.

87   *RONR* recognizes that a member holds a "duty" to vote in support or opposition of a motion. Yet, without detailed explanation, *RONR* also states that a member has a "right" to abstain because a member cannot be "compelled to vote." See *RONR* §45:3, page 385.

88   Here, a vote "prevented by law" will arise from a Member's conflict of interest or from state or local laws governing participation and voting due to the form of government (e.g., a mayor's statutory requirement to vote only in the event of a tie where a local ordinance limits the mayor's powers). Because conflicts of interest as well as limitations imposed by the form of government may be rules and requirements specific to the Body and its purpose, these matters should be addressed in the bylaws and not in the parliamentary procedures or rules of order for a meeting.

89   The Body's bylaws, code of ethics, or other policy may also recognize a Member's failure to follow Rule 7.4 and to vote "yes" or "no" as an intentional breach of the rules of order that may subject the Member to a specified disciplinary action, such as censure.

90   See, e.g., State ex rel. Miller v. Marshall, 184 So. 870 (1938) (finding that abstentions and nonvoting members "virtually acquiesce" in the decision made by those who do vote, citing numerous judicial decisions and tracing the common law to the 1760 decision of Oldknow v. Wainwright, 2 Burr. 1017 (English Reports, Full Print, Vol. 97, page 683)); 63 A.L.R.3d

1072 – *Abstentions from Voting of Member of Municipal Councils Present at Session as Affecting Results* ("courts have adopted and applied the rule or view that abstention is to be considered as acquiescence in [the] action favored by the majority of those who do vote, and have held or recognized that the nonvoting members should be considered, or counted, as having voted in the affirmative—in favor, that is, of the particular proposition requiring such a specific majority."); E. McQuillin, *The Law of Municipal Corporations*, § 13:46 (3rd edition, 2019) ("while it has been said that those present who refuse to vote for a proposition cannot be counted, the general rule is that they are regarded as having voted affirmatively, i.e., for the proposition ... a 'pass' vote must be counted as voting with the majority.").

91   See Chapter 3, Section 2.0, for the rules governing the quorum.

92   See C.R.S. § 31-16-103 for general municipal action by ordinance, resolution, or order and C.R.S., § 30-15-404 for general county action by ordinance.

93   Note that the Colorado Open Meetings Law (COML) requires this same voting standard as a matter of statutory law be applicable to every public body as defined by COML. See C.R.S. § 24-6-402(4).

94   See C.R.S. § 31-16-103.

95   See C.R.S. § 31-16-104.

96   See C.R.S. § 31-16-105.

97   See C.R.S. § 31-23-305.

98   See Section 22.0 and Colorado Open Meetings Law at C.R.S. § 24-6-402(4).

99 See Home Rule Charter for the City of Centennial, Colorado, §13.2 at https://library.municode.com/co/centennial/codes/municipal_code.

100 This objection should be raised by a Point of Order. See Section 11.0.

101 An idiom meaning that something more powerful is controlled by something less powerful. https://www.merriam-webster.com/words-at-play/wag-the-dog-idiom-meaning.

102 The number and names of classes of motions in *Bob's Rules of Order* differ from other procedural rules. For example, *RONR* provides five different classes of motions: main, subsidiary, privileged, incidental, and motions to bring a matter again before the assembly.

103 A Motion to Continue or Postpone is a hybrid motion, meaning that it can serve as a main motion or as a subordinate motion. As a main motion, the Motion to Continue or Postpone can be used to delay consideration of an item on an agenda that is not yet open or delay consideration of a matter that is open but for which no main motion is pending before the Body. As a subordinate motion, the Motion to Continue or Postpone will ask to delay a matter for which a main motion is on the Floor and pending before the Body.

104 See note 103.

105 A Member may use the phrase "Point of Clarification." The Presiding Officer should recognize that a Point of Information and a Point of Clarification are interchangeable.

106 See note 103.

107 The debatable motions are: Principal Motion, Continue or Postpone, Amend, Reconsider, and Adjourn.

108 The motions that are not debatable and are single-purpose motions are: Close Debate, Recess, and to conduct an Executive Session. A Motion to Amend, although debatable, is not capable of amendment pursuant to Rule 14.3 (no amendment of a motion to amend).

109 Other rules of order, including *RONR*, recognize a larger number of different main motions available to propose a general business action to the Body. The names of these general action motions include a "main motion," "original main motion," and "incidental main motion," among others. *Bob's Rules of Order* dispenses with a need to understand and differentiate between these varying and potentially confusing forms of main motions and simply recognizes that a Principal Motion is the form of main motion used to propose that the Body take an action.

110 An emergency ordinance will take effect immediately upon adoption. See C.R.S. § 31-16-105.

111 See C.R.S. § 31-23-305.

112 To understand the interchangeable nature of the terms "continue" and "postpone," see Chapter 2, Special Terminology, "Continue" and "Postpone."

113 Recall that "open" is defined by the *Rules* to mean that the agenda item has been formally announced or presented to the Body. See Chapter 2, Terminology, "Open."

114 See Section 9.0 to understand the priority of main, subordinate, and privileged motions.

115 A public notice customarily requires information that is sufficient to advise the public of the time, date, place, and purpose of the meeting or hearing.

116 See Chapter 2, Special Terminology, "Legislative," "Quasi-Judicial," and "Administrative Powers."

117 *Bob's Rules of Order* disfavors the use of the expression "call the question." This expression can create confusion because it can imply—and some bodies improperly allow the use of the expression in practice—to mandate the immediate cessation of debate and an immediate vote on the question (or motion). No published set of procedural rules authorizes a member to unilaterally stop the body's debate and cause a vote on a pending motion. The proper practice is to seek approval of the body to stop (i.e., close) debate, which, if approved, will naturally result in the motion proceeding to a vote. Nevertheless, the Presiding Officer can recognize a Member's intent behind a "motion to call the question" as a Motion to Close Debate. The *Rules* does not prohibit a Body's use of a motion to call the question if the use of the motion is ingrained in the Body's meeting practice.

118 See Chapter 2, Special Terminology, "Quasi-Judicial," "Legislative," and "Administrative Powers."

119 For a judicial decision noting the important differences between a motion to reconsider and motion to rescind a prior decision (under *RONR*), see L.C. Canyon Partners v. Salt Lake County, 266 P.3d 797 (Utah 2011).

120 Note that Rule 2.5 authorizes Members of the Body and administrative staff members to announce the adjournment of a meeting in the absence of a quorum.

121   A Point of Appeal challenging the Presiding Officer's discretionary decision to adjourn could be possible where the Body seeks to consider other non-agenda matters and the Presiding Officer uses the discretion to adjourn the meeting as a means of avoiding such consideration.

122   Recall that a Point of Information is privileged and is in order at any time and that any Member, including the Presiding Officer, my propose a Point of Information.

123   Here, the Town Attorney further understands that a motion that is not on the Floor can be voluntarily withdrawn by the Moving Member. See Rules 5.4 and 5.5.

124   Note that the Presiding Officer makes a motion in this example notwithstanding that Rule 3.5 encourages the Presiding Officer to customarily defer to the Members to take such action. Here, however, the Presiding Officer recognizes the efficiency of making the motion in order to directly inform the Body of the proposed process to most effectively adjourn the meeting.

125   Which authorization will be found at subsections (a) through (h) of C.R.S. § 24-6-402(4).

126   C.R.S. § 24-6-402(4).

127   Id.

128   C.R.S. § 24-6-402(4)(a).

129   C.R.S. § 24-6-402(4)(b).

130   C.R.S. § 24-6-402(4)(c).

131   C.R.S. § 24-6-402(4)(d).

132   C.R.S. § 24-6-402(4)(e).

133 C.R.S. § 24-6-402(4)(f)(I).

134 C.R.S. § 24-6-402(4)(f)(II).

135 Id. As a side note, a special statutory provision of the Colorado Open Meetings Law found at C.R.S. § 24-6-402(3.5) may authorize non-public executive sessions to conduct some of the business associated with selecting the government's chief executive officer (commonly the principal manager or administrator). Consultation is advised with the Body's legal counsel to understand the applicability of this statutory provision and the steps necessary to hold these very special forms of non-public public meetings.

136 C.R.S. § 24-6-402(4)(f)(II).

137 C.R.S. § 24-6-402(4)(g).

138 C.R.S. § 24-6-402 (2)(d.5)(II)(C).

139 C.R.S. § 24-6-402(9)(b).

140 Millage v. Spahn, 175 P.2d 982 (Colo. 1946) (a waiver is the intentional abandonment of a known right). Although an intent to waive a benefit may be implied by conduct, the conduct itself should be free from ambiguity and clearly manifest the intention not to assert the benefit. Department of Health v. Donahue, 690 P.2d 243, 247 (Colo. 1984).

141 The Colorado Open Meetings Law does not define the term "leadership." The *Rules of Order* subscribes to the proposition that "leadership" is a position on the Body that holds a present or potential future right to preside over the Body's meetings. Such position is customarily titled as mayor, mayor pro tem, council or board president or vice president, or chairperson or vice chairperson. The Body's legal counsel should be consulted

regarding the proper meaning of the term "leadership" and to consider the intent underlying the use of this undefined term in the Colorado Open Meetings Law at C.R.S. § 24-6-402(2)(d) (IV).

142 See note 141.

143 A "secret ballot" means "a vote cast in such a way that the identity of the person voting, or the position taken in such vote is withheld from the public." C.R.S. § 24-6-402(2)(d)(IV). For the purposes of the *Rules*, such methods may include but are not limited to the use of paper ballots without a designation of the person casting the vote or a form of voting software that allows the casting of anonymous votes.

144 In addition to holding a roll-call vote or by immediately posting each individual Member's vote, a vote will be deemed a publicly known vote if the vote is (i) cast on a written ballot, (ii) the written ballot clearly identifies the name of the voting Member, and (iii) the ballot is readily available for public inspection upon request.

145 Section 24.0 may be the preferred election process when the multiple positions to be filled each have different terms of office.